Emotional Poems

*How We Live and
How We Die.
Some Will Make You Think,
Others Will Make You Cry.*

George L. Hand

iUniverse, Inc.
Bloomington

EMOTIONAL POEMS
How We Live and How We Die. Some Will Make
You Think, Others Will Make You Cry.

iUniverse books may be ordered through booksellers or by contacting:
iUniverse
1663 Liberty Drive
Bloomington, IN 47403
www.iuniverse.com
1-800-Authors (1-800-288-4677)

ISBN: 978-1-4759-8078-3 (sc)
ISBN: 978-1-4759-8079-0 (e)

Printed in the United States of America

iUniverse rev. date: 3/15/2013

Dedication

I dedicate this book to the greatest, my wife.
For all these years we've had a terrific life.
Plus our kids and their spouses
Douglas and Kerstin Hand
Michael and Carol Hand
Jeffrey and Ann Hand
Courtenay and Barry McGrory

Acknowledgment

Most of these poems are fictional you'll find.
Conceived by the author's imaginative mind.
However, real live stories are represented here.
The connection to specific people is never clear.
There are poems about notable events making the news.
These are in the public domain in my view.
I want to thank all who have told me a tale
About the human condition. We try and we fail.
For all of you who have taken life's blows,
Most have been resilient as you and God know.
Finally, if you liked my poems and told me that fact,
I appreciate your response. It's great to get feedback.

Introduction

Through the millennia mankind has suffered a lot.
Predators, famine, and pestilence each gave us a shot.
The first two of these are not problems for now.
Microbes and viruses will always be with us somehow.
Between mutations and new ones, they will prevail.
Add to these the dozens of ways our bodies can fail.
If this isn't enough, our fellow man will give us a whack.
With terrorists, fanatics, and criminals we can't turn our back.
The fates are as bad, the wrong place and time.
This is the soldiers' lament and victims of crime.
Of course, we can be the cause of our own doom,
And society's stupidities can add to the gloom.
Will our lot improve as the future unfolds?
Some trends make me uneasy if truth be told.
However, I am the result of tens of thousands of forebears.
Each survived through a life full of cares.
Since they survived, then by God I can do the same.
Every person on this earth can make this claim.
Most of these poems are sad tales of woe.
You'll think there for the grace of God, I go.
Some tales are based on true stories I've heard.
Some are figments in both fact and word.
The final poems are included to give you a lift.
The human spirit will triumph. This is God's gift.

Table of Contents

Chapter 1

**Psychos and bullies have no
empathy. They don't care.
Of other's feelings they're just not aware.**

1. Tucson (or Anyplace*)

He came in the door. It was a political meeting.
No one knew him, so there was no greeting.
He went right up where the Representative stood.
He raised his pistol and thought, "This should be good."
Shot at point blank range, one bullet's enough.
Now he began shooting randomly, "I've got the right stuff."
Two old men pushed their wives to the floor,
And covered them with their bodies. They couldn't do more.
Suddenly came quiet. Empty, time to reload.
Self preservation should prevail. Run for the road.
This didn't happen with this diverse group.
Several converged on the madman in one fell swoop.
One unknown smashed a folding chair across his back.
Another twisted his arm to stop the attack.
A lady grabbed his ammo clip and tore it away.
Two men crashed onto his chest and legs in the foray.
A young man outside, heard shots and ran in.
Rather than taking off, no thought of his own skin.
He cradled the Rep's head to stem the blood flow.
Maybe he saved her life. No one will ever know.
When the cops arrived, it was time to take stock.

Six dead, thirteen wounded, all from one Glock.
One old man took two, and his wife died.
He wasn't successful, but by God he tried.
It was better for the other old man as it was his intent.
His wife's life was saved while his own was spent.
Another elderly woman, and the Congresswoman's aide,
A judge who just came by, all died in the raid.
The worst of all from that killing spree
Was a nine year old girl, just as innocent as can be.
Her interest in politics was why she was there.
Maybe in twenty years she would have occupied that chair.
The Representative survived her devastating wound.
What will the future bring? Has her life been ruined?
People ask, how could this madman have slipped through
the cracks.
No one blew the whistle to preempt his attack.
Unfortunately, in our society, we can't arrest for what might be,
And mental hospitals have to let people go free,
Unless they're a threat to themselves or others,
Which no one can tell, even their fathers or mothers.
All in all, from this disaster, what did we learn?
Heroic people step forward at every turn.
Their duty as human beings, they'll never spurn.
*Why? Because it's my hope that anywhere people will
act heroically.

2. Stolen

Traveling to Europe had been the girls' dream.
It's just as safe as the USA or so it seems.
Big cities where the natives are sophisticated and nice,
Especially Paris, people may be naughty, but there's little vice.

The girls were naive. What could happen here?
Busy airport, city streets, fancy hotel, what's to fear?
Little did they know how organized the criminals were.
Spotted getting off the plane, they caused a stir.
Two attractive, innocent, American blonds and young,
Alert the chain, these lovelies will soon be sprung.
A handsome young man walked with them to the taxi stand.
They started loading their baggage. He gave a hand.
"These taxis are really expensive, could we share a ride?
I'm familiar with Paris. On the trip I can be a guide."
This was acceptable especially with this charming guy.
He proposed, "There's going to be a party tonight nearby.
I'll give you a call and then if you decide to go,
I can give you directions, and we'll make it so.
Give me your room number. I'll call in an hour or two."
Sounds pretty innocent. The girls didn't have a clue.
They settled in and took showers and naps.
One woke up when she heard a door rap.
She didn't have time to react or even scream.
Her mouth was covered by a member of the pick up team.
Both girls were placed in laundry hampers and sedated
They were covered and wheeled to where a truck waited.
This is one story that would not have a happy end.
They were auctioned to a wealthy man with money to spend.
Spirited out of the country, they wound up in a harem somewhere.
Being drugged or beaten, rebellion they wouldn't dare.
When their owner became bored, he sold them away.
This continued until they entered a brothel one day.
The last stop was when they became too old.
An unmarked grave awaited. They no longer could be sold.
Parents take heed of the narrative here told.

3. Abduction

"They surprised me and knocked me to the ground.
Miguel is missing. He's nowhere to be found.
I would have fought to the death to save my child.
There's nothing more dangerous than a mother gone wild."
"Senora, we will search all over the state.
Notices will be sent, but I think it's too late.
These banditos plan kidnapping with care.
They grab a child, then quickly get out of there.
I hate to say it, but there's little likelihood
Of getting Miguel back. The chances aren't good."
(Besides, who gives a damn about your neighborhood.)
So another child is put up for adoption.
The well off seeking one, settle for this option.
When they are willing to pay the big bucks,
The unscrupulous will make sure they have good luck.
Some poor family suffers. This system sucks.

4. Roofies

"Hey Ruthie, want to go to a party tonight.
It's at the Sigma house. It should be all right.
I met a guy, and he said to bring a friend.
He claimed nobody would push any booze if that offends.
I know you promised your folks you wouldn't drink.
This seems innocent enough. That's what I think."
The two girls entered the frat. All seemed cool.
Some were playing pinball, and some were playing pool.
In the back room a few couples were dancing.
Others were wrapped up with each other romancing.
"Can I get you ladies a drink, whatever you like?
I'm sort of the bartender. My name's Mike."

"I'll have a Coke or Pepsi, and I'll pour my own."
Ruthie was careful. She'd never leave her drink alone.
Later her friend disappeared. She hoped all was well.
They were to watch out for each other. It had been a spell.
Ruthie dropped her guard as she looked around the room.
A deft hand dosed her drink. She was doomed.
She downed the Coke. Then her life became a blank.
The next day she had no recollection of the prank.
She realized she had been raped. She had clues.
She hurt in private places. She smelled different too.
Ruthie did what many girls would not do.
She went to the police and explained what she'd been through.
A kindly police woman explained roofies to her.
This drug kills your memory. Everything becomes a blur.
Plus, there's no way to determine who did the deed.
Unless you can match DNA, the only way to proceed.
No judge would go along on such a fishing expedition,
Namely, testing every frat male which is against legal tradition.
The cops would do nothing to help poor Ruth,
And the college administration also needed proof.
Stop action. Ruth told her folks. Their relationship was true love.
Dad was a powerful lawyer and push came to shove.
He organized all the parents and legislative friends.
They all decided this treatment of girls had to end.
Result. The fraternity house was closed in perpetuity.
Every member was expelled because of complicity.
The university president was fired along with the dean of men.
Suits were launched all over, so this would never happen again

5. Wife Beater

When they were young, they seemed truly in love.
It was as if their union was blessed from above.
All the moms thought Jim was such a nice guy.
Polite, outgoing, charming, attentive is why.
They told their girls they should find one like him.
They all missed one aspect that made life grim.
Jim really wanted to control his future spouse.
His charm covered up that he was a louse.
When they were courting, he called several times a day.
Normal guys don't want to dominate your time that way.
Marriage followed. The "attentiveness" got worse.
He kept track of the car mileage and control of the purse.
Jim made sure the wife's time was accounted for.
He didn't even want her to go out the door.
Any little thing "wrong", he'd go into a rage.
Soon the hitting started. That was the next stage.
Jim had ultimate control. His wife lived in fear.
He made her so dependent, she couldn't get clear.
Where could she run? Where could she hide?
He kept the car keys and money by his side.
People often wonder why a wife stays with such a cad.
She is so dependant, she thinks a new life will be just as bad.
Then the very worst happens one day,
He kills her in his rage or it's the other way.
So dear ladies, there's a warning that I must tell,
If a guy is too charming and attentive, run like hell.

6. The Drunk

Some drunks get happy. They fall asleep if they have too much.
There's no danger unless they drive. Booze is their crutch.

They will drink up the money, leave their family poor,
And will ruin their health, early death for sure.
Then there's the nasty drunk who can make life hell.
They're aggressive in person and behind the wheel as well.
They'll look for a fight. Stay out of their path.
Even women and children will feel their wrath.
"Jimmy, Daddy just got home. Quick, hide.
Not in the closet. He'll find us if he looks inside.
Under the bed. Maybe he won't look there.
God, please protect Mom. Help her take care."
"Damn it, Joe, you're drunk. Stay away from me."
"Where's the boys? They need a lesson, see.
And listen, bitch. Don't tell me what to do.
Looks like I need to teach you a lesson too."
When you're drunk, your balance is not so good.
Joe swung, missed and fell as his wife knew he would.
She had enough practice and knew when to duck.
Today she would avoid black eyes if she had any luck.
Joe slept off his drunk on the kitchen floor.
It's a good bet the next day, he'd drink some more.
The family made a decision that very night.
They'd leave their home. With a few boxes they'd take flight.
There are shelters for families who live in fear
With secret locations so the abuser can't come near.
Their alternative is the prospect of death.
One or another would take his last breath.

7. Good Samaritan (GS)

GS, "That poor guy, he looks okay, no need to take care.
You've got a flat. Do you have a jack and a spare?"
Perp, "I do, but also the damn thing won't start.

Do you have a phone? Mine's dead. I'm not too smart."
GS, "Sure do, but first let me look under the hood.
Maybe it's something simple. That would be good."
P, "Don't bother. Just hand over your keys.
Also, I'll take your wallet and phone if you please.
They warn Good Samaritans about people like me.
You should have listened, I think you'll agree."
GS, "Could you just take the money and credit cards.
Replacing most of that stuff will be exceedingly hard."
P, "Forget about it. Now if you're wise, you won't remember my face.
Unless you want a bullet before I leave this place."
Wow, how wrong can a good turn go.
It's much too late to say, I told you so.

8. Rage

"Sir, show me your license and registration please.
Now, out of the car, slowly, don't even sneeze.
Spread your legs and lean against the hood.
I'm going to cuff you. You best be good."
"Officer, what's going on? Could you please explain."
"Sure, you left an accident. People thought you were insane.
Witnesses saw you side swipe and push a car off the road.
A lot of vehicles were damaged in this episode.
One old guy had a heart attack and may not live.
Personally, I hope you get the max the law has to give."
"But officer, I was justified. He wouldn't move out of my way.
I was in a hurry. He was ruining my day.
They should keep old geezers off the road by law.
If I get punished, the system has a flaw."
"Duck your head and climb in the back seat.

Tell your story to the judge who you'll soon meet.
The difference between insanity and road rage blurs.
Too bad they can't test for attitudes like yours.
I'd never let you drive unless you had a certified cure."

9. Mean Kids

What happens to kids along the way?
They're sweet as infants and toddlers you can say.
We have worked with kids in the early grades.
They treat each other well, kindness doesn't fade.
Something happens later in elementary school or junior high,
Some seem to get a nasty streak. I don't know why.
They'll decide they don't like one of the gals or guys.
Any differences they can spot, they really despise.
Pick on him for where he lives or the clothes he wears,
His skin color or body build or the length of his hair.
This is bullying and the bully has his clique.
Most of the victims seem to be meek.
Back in ancient times, "in loco parentis" was the rule,
Meaning teachers could act like parents in school.
Somehow you'd think the teachers would know,
And they could stop bullying before there are blows.
Don't parents know when their kids act this way?
Do they want them thinking bullying is okay?
Maybe both teachers and parents are just afraid
The bullies will go after them if too much trouble is made.
The result can be catastrophic, all outcomes bad.
The victim's life is ruined, and he goes quite mad.
He kills himself or retaliates which is worse,
Or the bully never learns and prison is his curse.

10. Deadly Reaction

"Well, another school year is about to start.
Maybe it will be better. I have to take heart.
The damn bullies can really get me down.
They haven't beaten me up. They just act the clown.
Sneak up behind and knock my books to the floor,
Or trip me from behind walking through the door.
They all laugh at the nerd, what a sight.
Maybe it's their way to pick a fight.
I remember each one. This year I'll have my day.
I can picture the surprise when I blow them away.
Not in school, I'm too smart for that.
I'll get them outside. I'll strike like a cat.
I have a repeating rifle. I practice a lot.
At a hundred feet I can hit a melon with each shot.
I can reload quickly. I've practiced speed.
No one stands a chance when I do my deed.
They'll find out who's defenseless and weak.
I will give them one warning before my gun speaks."
Wouldn't it be smart to avert this reactive ploy
By stopping the bullies from tormenting a quiet boy.

11. The Camp Survivor

I guess I have the right to be depressed.
Though of my possible life outcomes, I got the best.
I was barely a teenager when they took me away.
My Aunt Hilda's house was where I had stayed.
She was married to a Christian. Her husband was at war.
The records were lost. There never was a knock on the door.
Then early in forty five someone squealed.
Maybe for better treatment, a neighbor made a deal.

I was taken while Hilda was killed on the spot.
Jews evading capture infuriated the Nazis, and so she was shot.
Somehow we had managed to get enough to eat,
More than a starvation diet, but without any meat.
I tell you this so you'll know how I could survive.
With the truck and cattle car ride, my reserve kept me alive.
The guards saw that I could work when we met,
So I wasn't assigned to the showers just yet.
That's what they called the gas chambers, but we knew.
No one ever returned which certainly was a clue.
I sorted the victims' shoes and clothes with care.
Stuff that was okay, worn out, or needing repair.
I worked at other jobs too horrible to mention,
But I survived my concentration camp detention.
Survived for what. I realized my entire family was gone.
No wishful thinking, no prayers, no new day with the dawn.
I got some real help from an American GI.
I was put on a ship that headed west by and by.
They found a distant cousin in New York City.
He raised me and educated me. It was family, not pity.
Life has been good, but I'll never forget.
My dreams are filled with that horror yet.
Will it ever end? I'm afraid of getting old.
You lose recent memories, while the rest are still sharp I'm told.
Why couldn't Alzheimers reverse this hold?

12. Narcissism

She, "Come see all the new outfits I bought.
I've looked all over. They're what I've really sought.
I'll try them on. Tell me how pretty I look.
Some were bargains, You won't believe the effort it took?

I got some new cosmetics. I'm tired of the old stuff.
You know what they say? You can never have enough."
He, "Dear, we're headed for trouble. You've maxed out
the cards.
Paying our bills this month will be hard.
You know the closets are full of all your things.
Couldn't you wear those instead of taking a fling."
She, "Oh, fiddle faddle. I can't wear those rags.
I want to look good, not like some old hag."
Later, after studying herself for a while.
She, "Something's not right with my face when I smile.
I think I should see that plastic surgeon I met.
He can make me look better I bet."
She later, "I just did my face and fixed my hair.
I'm not in the mood, so don't you dare."
He later, "You've got to stop. Creditors call all the time."
She, "So earn more money. You could even turn to crime."
This young lady is uninterested in others, only self counts.
She'll never be satisfied while the family's debt mounts.
When they no longer have credit, she'll drop her guy.
She'll find someone else to support her by and by.
Maybe a sugar daddy will pick her as a trophy wife.
Then she'll spend as she wishes and have that great life.
The lesson here for both female and male,
Stay clear of narcissists. Any love will always fail.
They can only love themselves. All other love pales.

13. Phone Scam

The department store's computer had been breached.
None knew how much credit information had been reached.
Would the hackers sell card numbers and names?

People had to be warned before disaster came.
Within hours telephones started to ring.
Callers explained about the hacking thing.
Then, "We have the problem solved. In this regard,
To make sure, would you read me the number of your card.
Also, to verify that you are truly you,
Would you read me your social security number too."
Stop. Never tell numbers over the phone to any man.
When they call you and ask, you know it's a scam.

14. The Scam

"Hello, you'll have to speak loud. I can't hear so well."
"Grandma, Grandma, it's your grandson. Remember me, Mel.
I'm in real trouble. They have me in jail.
I'll have to stay here unless I make bail.
I can't call my folks. They'll have a fit.
I know Dad won't help. It's that responsibility bit.
I'm supposed to be an adult and take my lumps.
It's a really big mistake, and I'm in the dumps."
"There, there, I'll help you out as much as I can.
How much do you need? What's the plan?"
"I need twenty four hundred." Notice the amount.
It's not too much and not an even count.
"Mel" knows exactly what to say.
He can direct a money transfer his way.
If Grandma responds and sends the cash,
She'll be hit up for more, the scammer is so brash.
He has done his homework well you see.
He knows all the names and the probability.
This is one of the worst type of scams,
Since it victimizes the kindly, elderly Grams.

Grandma, before sending money should make one call.
Her own child will know if she should stall.
Mel may even be home and can come to the phone.
The scam's exposed though the impostor will never be known.
A safe bet for the old or young to do,
Is never send money when someone calls you.

15. Old Civilization

Some civilizations have been around ever so long.
Because they've lasted, maybe they do nothing wrong.
At least that's the theory. From them we should learn,
Improve our western ways by giving another way a turn.
For instance the Chinese revere their old.
Take care of them, their wisdom is gold.
What a great thought, but this requires a loving son.
Thus, daughters have no worth and so are shunned.
In olden days when a woman was about to give birth,
A drowning bucket took care of a baby with no worth.
Now to determine gender, there's ultrasound.
An abortion takes care of the problem they've found.
I don't know how any woman can go along with this,
Nor any man who loves mother, daughter, wife or sis.
By and large I'll take our ways of doing things.
Unintended consequences are what outside ideas bring.

16. The Law

The child was outside playing. It was such a nice day.
In another year she wouldn't be able to go out that way.
Religious law requires she be accompanied by a man,
But only her dad or brother or a close member of her clan.
That day an evil man grabbed her from the street.

He raped her though she was so young and sweet.
She cried to her Mom who told her Dad.
They knew the rapist, the worst kind of cad.
Dad decided they must go to the religious court.
The judge who heard the story was the strictest sort.
He made his decision based on religious law.
The punishment was public stoning, but there's a flaw.
The young girl was led to the local arena.
Townspeople gathered as if served a subpoena.
They all brought their stones to do their part.
No one asked the question before the start.
No Jesus said, "Let he without sin, cast the first stone."
A thousand did their duty, and she died alone.
How can anyone, anywhere, this punishment condone?

17. No Rights

Here we are in modern times. Life should be good.
However, part of the world has its own "should."
There, the female half of the population has no rights,
Unlike in the "west" where most countries have seen the light.
A young woman can not be seen in a public place
Without covering all her body including her face.
She can't go many places without an escorting male,
That's her husband, father, or brother without fail.
She should walk slowly and quietly lest the police see.
For any infraction, she'll be beaten by legal decree.
A girl cannot attend school, her education is spurned.
She'll never be able to read lest in secret learned.
For all women, forget about medical treatment or care.
No male doctor can touch her. No women practice there.
She has no choice, a husband is picked for her.

He can get a divorce. She doesn't get to concur.
He gets all the property, the money, the kids.
No support, no alimony, of her he is completely rid.
Since no business or property, she can own,
She can't inherit anything. She's all alone.
A few examples worse than being accosted and hit,
Uncovered young girls have had their throats slit.
Women or girls who have suffered from rape,
Have been honor killed by brothers with no escape.
A man when asked about a trip to the market by his wife,
Said, "If she didn't get my permission, I must take her life."
A women who went to court to stop a harassing guy,
Got twelve lashes. She wasn't accompanied is why.
If I were a women there, I'd rather be a slave or die.
Is this modern times? Have 1400 years gone by?

18. Little Joy

"Hey Sarge, we just came back from patrol.
We're supposed to be nice. Live up to our role.
Young boys like soldiers. They were hanging around.
Something happened that truly astounds.
I handed one of the kids a soccer ball.
He wouldn't touch it and then hid behind a wall."
"This is your first tour. You haven't been here long.
I'll tell you about things, so you won't do anything wrong.
These strict Muslims are a strange lot.
Most everything we like, they just do not.
First of all, education is just for the boys.
They can't play games. I don't think there's any toys.
Music, singing, and sports are not allowed.
No photography, no painting, no TV, anything pretty is under a shroud.

Forget entertainment with dancing, liquor, or cards.
Life here is bleak, and they make it really hard.
If that boy had taken the ball, you know,
He would have been beaten with a lot of blows.
None of us can imagine a life without fun.
That's why we wonder, almost every one,
What the hell are we doing here. We should be done."

19. Religious Police

She was a foreigner in this religious land.
She learned all the rules. Adherence they demand.
Wear foot length dresses and cover arms and face.
How can they survive the heat in this place?
She worked in the consulate. Her status should count.
However, stuff happens, to her an unreasonable amount.
A gust of wind blew her dress askew
Bringing her bare ankles and calves into view.
They have religious police to check on what won't do.
They're also judge, jury, and executioners too.
This cop had to show the foreign born chick.
He beat her severely with his punishment stick.
She got back to the consulate and saw the guys.
They were incensed, so much they planned a surprise.
All the baseball bats in the consulate were found.
They then went hunting. It was fertile ground.
Each religious policeman they came upon then
Was soundly beaten by those pissed off men.
I never found out the result of this foray.
I suppose all involved were sent on their way.
I hope the religious cops learned a lesson that day.

20. The Second Day of Infamy

Our country had been branded by those across the sea.
The "Great Satan" was our designation, not the land of the free.
We are nothing but infidels as well as Israel's friend.
Therefore, we should be punished to the very end.
A group was formed by the most fanatical of the day.
To make war on all infidels but especially the USA.
They knew there's no way to beat us face to face,
So they learned to use bombs set almost any place.
A giant building was attacked, bombed at its base.
People were killed, but there was little damage in that space.
Embassies were next, those in African nations.
Here they had no care about international relations.
Finally, they'd show the Great Satan and hatched a plan.
They found 20 volunteers, each a fanatical man.
Finances were no problem, the Saudis had the wealth.
They willingly paid protection, safeguarding their own health.
Passports and cash were provided to the men.
They easily gained entry to our country and then
Several were accepted at commercial flying schools.
This raised no suspicion. In retrospect we were fools.
A witticism, "We only want to learn flying skills.
We don't need any takeoff or landing drills."
These terrorists found air routes satisfying their desires.
With early departures and full fuel tanks to stimulate fires.
They picked their targets, the two World Trade Towers,
The Pentagon, and the Capitol Building, symbols of our powers.
The date was September 11 of 2001,
Precisely 60 years since the Pentagon was begun.
Maybe the date was chosen by accident, maybe with care,

When we hear nine eleven or nine, one, one our memories
are there.
Four aircraft were boarded. The terrorists did their deed.
The second Day of Infamy, patriots take heed.

21. Nine Eleven

"That plane is really loud. Should we take a look?
Hear that crash? Good God, the building shook.
I don't like this. Someone call downstairs.
It's smoke I see out the window there.
That plane hit our building, what a blow.
I remember that happened some fifty years ago.
A two engine military plane hit the Empire State.
The low cloud ceiling sealed their fate.
Except for visibility, maybe that happened here.
Hope nobody died and the damage's not too severe.
They called from downstairs, stay where we are.
The fireman will climb up. It's awfully far.
I'll call home and tell them I'm okay.
Damn, there's no answer. The wife's away.
I can smell smoke, and it's starting to get hot.
Some people are praying. They're crying a lot.
Come on. Check the exit. Can we get up the stairs?
Close it quickly. It's smokey and like an oven out there.
What was that flashing by the window? Oh no,
Somebody jumped. He chose the quick way to go.
I hear rumbling. The floor's starting to shake.
Dear Lord, help us all for our family's sake.
I believe in you, Jesus. Please forgive me..."
Red hot steel loses its strength you see.
No design error or construction flaw

Caused the great building to obey gravity's law.
When you weaken support, the building goes down.
Four hundred thousand tons will crash to the ground.
It probably made no difference which way people died,
Instantaneously after an eight second fall or crushed
alive.
The perps were successful, more than they had thought.
Do we need a bigger lesson to be taught,
That this was a declaration of war on their part.
Though too many have made excuses from the start.
Remember, there was dancing in the streets after this attack,
So never forget who did it, some day they'll get it back.

22. Rescue

"I don't know how we can put this fire out.
For burning liquids foam is best, no doubt.
That's what they use at airports for a crash.
Trucks are ready to go. They get there in a flash.
Water is all we have if we get up to the fire.
Carrying all this equipment up stairs, I'm starting to tire.
I keep thinking about design, what they could have done.
Who would have figured this? I'd say no one.
I'd have put a big tank of water way up top.
To flood any floor with automatic starts and stops.
This wouldn't extinguish this fire, but cooling it is good.
Maybe keep it from spreading as it usually would.
Why am I doing this? I could have retired last year,
Find a low stress job, nothing you'd call a career.
Well, after this, it's time to hang up the spurs.
I'll tell the young bucks, the job is all yours.
We got everyone out from the lowest stories.

Now comes the hard part when we earn the glory.
I hear rumbling. The building's starting to shake.
What's happening? Have we had it for goodness sake?"
So ended another life, instantaneous or just about.
410 other rescue workers' lives were so snuffed out.
The big city firemen's job, I've always read
Is the most dangerous with more winding up dead.
For sure these men didn't sign up for this,
But they did their duty and none were remiss.

23. Flight 93*

"My God, I just got a call from my wife.
Planes crashed into the twin towers, big loss of life.
They suspect terrorists took control of the planes.
Maybe they flew them after all the crew were slain.
We have been told to let hijackers have their way.
Be calm, cool and collected and do what they say.
That's presuming they'll want us as hostages and land somewhere.
They'll make wild demands when we get there.
This is different. These guys have complete control.
They're going to crash us. Maybe Washington's their goal.
We should fight back if we're going to die anyway.
They're just armed with utility knives I'd say.
How many are with me? It's our last chance to fight.
We may be untrained, but by God it's right.
There's six of us. More will join seeing we have heart.
All ready? When I count three, we'll start."
Three pealed to the rear, three to the front.
They carried attache cases, the knives to blunt.

They made quick work of their terrorist guards.
With many fists and feet, it wasn't too hard.
The terrorist flight crew heard the melee in back.
The cabin door was locked to stop any attack.
Four men picked up a terrorist from the floor
And used him as a battering ram against the door.
Others searched for tools. An extinguisher was found.
This made a better object with which to pound.
The door was breached. Men crowded in.
It's thought the terrorists knew they couldn't win.
The plane wasn't on autopilot and was flying low.
On purpose they dove the plane toward the ground below.
Too late to experiment, only seconds to act,
Flight 93 hit the ground before our people could react.
Forty heroic men died instantly on that plane.
Because of them, countless others weren't slain.
Ordinary people do great things. It's so ordained.
*No one knows exactly what happened that day.
Maybe the description provided here is the way.

24. The Empty Box

Mom, he's coming back. We don't know he's dead.
We can always have hope. That's what you said.
I know that the great building crashed to the ground.
And people caught there have never been found.
Maybe Dad got out somehow. Let's think about it.
He climbed to the roof. Dad would use his wits.
He'd tie some rope to plastic sheets,
And make a parachute to drop to the street.
He'd see the Hudson River and steer that way.
A boat would find him before he reached the bay.

I've always hoped a helicopter got him off the roof.
We shouldn't give up hope 'til we have proof.
I won't believe he's dead though his funeral's today.
That empty box won't stop my hoping in any way.
My Dad will come home, I'll always pray.

Chapter 2

We don't need someone else's disdain.
We're quite capable of providing our own pain.

1. Final Day

My doc said I've got a month. That's the score.
Does he really know? Is it less or more?
They tell you that so you'll settle your affairs.
I've already made arrangements except for one care.
Marsha's been sick, but she'll get by.
She'll be financially okay when I die.
But there's no way she can care for our son, we agree.
For 40 years we've done it. His mental age is about three.
The state would warehouse him with impersonal care.
I can't bring myself to put him there.
Dear Lord, I hope I've chosen the right path.
If my sin is too big, I accept your wrath.
"Son, we'll get in the car. It's time to go.
I don't want Mom to hear, but she will know.
I left her a note to explain what I've done.
I've always loved you my poor needful son."
"Boom!" and now one more, and then I am done.

2. If You Only Knew

Oh, Bill, if you only knew
How much your family depended on you.
Business failures happen. That's part of life.

For richer or poorer, you took that vow with your wife.
Financial hardship is not an insurmountable hill.
Most of your kids could help with the bills.
The wife could take a part time job as well.
Nothing's wrong with all contributing for a spell.
You didn't wait to see how things would work out.
I know you weren't thinking, depression no doubt.
People all wondered why you did it.
There's no rational answer that will fit.
All depressed people should take note.
Your family loves and needs you. Give them a vote.

3. The Whistler

Going toward home, Mario walked down the street.
It was a lovely Spring day that he called sweet.
He liked to whistle, and he was quite good.
People enjoyed his music in the neighborhood.
He didn't hear the comments as he went by.
"Oh, Dear Lord, here he comes, so chipper and spry.
That poor boy, what will happen now?"
Mario was unaware but soon wrinkled his brow.
He saw several cars and wondered why.
He couldn't think no matter how he tried.
Then the lightning struck, the cause of his dread.
People were there because his sister was dead.
She had taken her own life. Were things that bad?
No one knows what makes another so sad.
Mario loved his sister. She was like the light of dawn.
There was no more whistling. The joy was gone.

4. Failing

"I wasn't doing so well back in school.
I think I'm smart enough. At least I'm not a fool.
Mom and especially Dad would get on my case.
My standard response was, get out of my face.
I'll never get into Yale. Well screw them.
Do I want to be like Dad? What a gem.
I hate school, and I would hate college too.
That's why I enlisted. It's the thing I want to do.
I'll be in the airborne and jump out of planes.
I'm sure to get to Korea and give my folks some pains."

"They sent me home. I got a medical discharge,
Due to that damn sergeant and the captain in charge.
They had some stupid head doctor there.
Gave me some tests. To hell with it, I don't care.
Now my folks are giving me another ration of crap.
Who wants this? It's like I'm in a trap.
The house is empty. Now is the time. I'm an action type guy.
Turn on the oven. Put my head in and goodbye."
This time he was successful and on the first try.

5. Gourmets

It's the way with living things, we all like to eat.
We need food to survive, so nature made it a treat.
Pain if we don't eat, pleasure if we do,
That's why it can easily be an addiction for the few.
The swings aren't as bad as for the heroin addict,
But the brain says eat more. That's its edict.
It's not always true, but these we can call epicures,
Gourmets, gourmands, maybe gluttons, or connoisseurs.

Food becomes the central goal of their lives.
Searching out the best restaurants is their drive.
They talk about food, where you get the very best.
Caviar, truffles, organically raised, and the rest.
Naturally, with all this effort they gain weight.
It's hard to restrict what they put on their plate.
I have a feeling there really is no cure.
Diets work while the restrictions they endure.
The gourmet doesn't realize a lifetime change is required.
Going back to the old ways means results most dire.
Thus, the dieters regain the lost pounds.
Going up is quicker than loss, it's found.
Even with restricting the stomach's size,
Lost weight is regained. This is not a surprise.
I must tell what happened to a lady we knew.
She had four kids and each time she grew.
As years passed she became really large.
She hired an immigrant lady to be in charge.
This women took complete care, nursed and cooked.
Her employer became bed ridden, to food she was hooked.
She could not get up, her weight was too great.
She finally died in bed, any help was too late.
Maybe killing taste buds, this addiction we could beat.
Then gourmets would eat to live rather than live to eat.

6. Diabetes

When I look back, I've had a good life.
I'm lucky as hell I found such a great wife.
She's stayed with me, and sometimes it was hard.
I can be quite moody when I let down my guard.
We raised two fine sons. They're doing okay.

Both are married with kids. They're well on their way.
I've worked hard and made a good living, I know.
Maybe not that good, since I don't have that much to show.
We always had enough. What more do you need?
There's one thing, all please take heed.
I wish that I'd taken better care of my health.
This is surely important, more important than wealth.
I have abused my body with eating too much.
All my adult life I've smoked and drank and such.
What makes me happy as my days get long,
I have been blessed to have a lady who's strong.
I've got diabetes in its advanced stage, you see.
I just had both legs amputated above the knee.
Soon that, with my blindness means an early end to my life.
That's why I'm glad I picked the lady I did for my wife.

7. Self Punishment

"Mommy, it hurts. Please don't stick me again.
I hate it. You just gave me a shot at ten."
The child has had diabetes from a very young age.
He gets pin pricks regularly, his blood sugar to gage.
This is necessary to determine the insulin amount.
Four shots in the gut is the normal daily count.
Sometimes he is brave, sometimes he'll cry.
Always he wonders that big question, why?
None of the kids he knows suffers this hell.
They only get sniffles. They are quite well.
Other kids can eat what they can take,
Ice cream, candy, cookies, and cake.
His folks carefully measure each treat for him.
Too much or too little sugar, and your chances dim,

Fainting resulting in a fall, diabetic coma, and death.
Later comes blindness, amputations, pain to your last breath.
Guess what happens in the teenage years.
Rebellion of the worst kind, what each parent fears.
He won't self test nor take an insulin dose.
He's punishing himself for being different than most.
If he survives this age, maybe he'll know the score.
This is what he was dealt. There is no more.
You only go this way once. Live with what you've got.
Life can still be beautiful despite the blot.

8. He Doesn't Make Me Happy

Sometimes married couples think of divorce.
Talking to a third party can help of course.
I'd like to point out a few things if I can.
It's better to talk separately to both woman and man.
When a couple gets older, some of the bloom wears off.
This is expected. We change with age, so don't scoff.
Neither is a 20 year old kid. You're more mature.
You need to think of your own kids' needs for sure.
Work takes time. Maybe more than you'd like.
You don't want the boss to say, "Take a hike."
I know both have big demands on your time
Much more so than when you were in your prime.
Keep all this in mind when you make a decision.
Maybe of your plans you'll make a revision.
Consider the question, "Will I be better off alone?"
Do your kids need both of you 'til they're full grown?
Will financial considerations be a problem for you?
The cost of households is much more for two.
Never think, "He doesn't make me happy. He makes me sad."

Only you can control your emotions, good or bad.
Think most of what you pledged at the start,
A series of vows, you should really take them to heart.

9. Divorce Hits All

"I wish those kids could have learned to get along.
They had some differences. Nothing was that wrong.
I know for sure they loved each other to start.
They're both healthy with no addictions and smart.
Bob was a good provider. They lived pretty well.
What caused this good life to turn into hell?
I have a feeling some just like to fight.
The other partner can never make it right.
It's gotten so bad that Marta hates his guts.
She'll definitely get the kids, no ifs, ands, or buts.
If Bob wants to see the kids, she's going to make it hard,
And she won't give an inch, much less a yard.
I guess she'll keep those three kids out of our sight.
Grandparents by law just have no rights.
She hates him so much, she's transferred it to us.
We share the blame, and we don't know what's the fuss.
We'll probably not see the grand kids again.
Everybody suffers, all the relatives, and even friends.
I wish couples would realize how many are hurt.
They could try harder, their breakup to avert."

10. Broken Pact

The old couple and their friends were eating out.
"Joe, please be careful," she said. It was more of a shout.
"Let me brush you off. You're a mess.
I should help you more with eating I guess."

Poor Joe is suffering from Parkinson's disease.
His muscles don't work well. It gets worse by degrees.
He has a tendency to spill things. He doesn't mean it.
His wife knows this. There's no need for a snit.
If their friends are offended, then it's tough.
You don't need such people. Of them you've had enough.
Any embarrassment is only made worse
When a spouse publicly chastises. It's almost a curse.
Everyone should know about Parkinson's, MS, and strokes.
The body self destructs. It's unfixable and broke.
The problem is, the husband made a pact,
To always be the strong, protective one to be exact.
His spouse is mad about this, though she's unaware.
She forgot the vow in sickness and health, to always care.
I make a plea. When your spouse is in need,
Don't lower his self respect more with a thoughtless deed.
It's your turn to take the family lead.

11. The Mom

When I was young, I decided what I wanted in life.
I didn't think career. I wanted to be a mother and wife.
I met Terry, and we hit it off okay.
Maybe I was settling, wishful thinking you could say.
Time was flying by, and it was time to get a man.
We married and had two kids. That was the plan.
I loved my little ones, a girl and a boy.
This is what I wanted, my life full of joy.
We bought a little house in a quiet little town.
This was ideal, a life of ups and no downs.
I was a good mom. I even made my babies' food.
As they grew, I taught them all that I could.

We had a garden, and I put away preserves.
For my kids, I provided all they deserved.
When they grew and were ready for high school,
I drove them to another town. The best was our rule.
Something happened as our kids grew, I can't explain.
Terry was never that nice, but he caused emotional pain.
He treated me like dirt, a person of no worth.
He turned my children. I'd loved them since birth.
The divorce went forward. The kids chose him.
They were brain washed. Their love just dimmed.
I got the house, but had to pay Terry half.
I had to provide half for college. The judge was daft.
How could I cope? I worked part time jobs.
Sometimes I couldn't take it. I'd lay down and sob.
Now my kids are out of college and on their own.
Their lives are screwed up. Who could have known?
Why me, Lord? Why did this get piled on my head?
I just wanted to be a mom. Sometimes I wish I were dead.
I'll keep plugging. Maybe it'll get better instead.

12. New Mother

I say, "It's that good food," when they ask about my weight.
I've been wearing loose fitting clothes of late.
I'll stay away. They won't know in my home town.
I told my Mom, which made her feel really down.
But I really feel so lonely up here.
There's no one I can talk to about my fears.
I guess it's better that no one is told.
Secrets travel. It only takes one scold.
Not even Alex knows what's happening here.
He's going to be a dad, but I don't want him near.

Alex keeps talking about coming to visit me.
I put him off, exams, term papers, I'm busy as a bee.
I won't abort. I'm going to go full term.
My baby will be adopted. On this I'm firm.

I didn't see the baby. That's what I had said.
Easier to separate myself from a future I'd dread.
That damn nurse. She told me it was a girl.
I hope the new parents treat her like a pearl.
She'll be beautiful. I know this for sure.
She'll grow up healthy and smart. Can I endure?
Stop it! Stop it! Not thinking is my only cure.

13. Not Enough Protection

A little exercise was tried with our youth group.
These were high school kids. We tried to give them the scoop.
We gave an oreo cookie to the first in line.
Lap it and pass it on. We looked for a good sign.
After the first one, no one would do it.
"Yuch! I'm not going to lap someone else's spit."
"Well kids, is there a lesson for us here?
Should you exchange bodily fluids with those you don't hold dear?
Aside from pregnancy which you can prevent with a pill,
There's sexually transmitted diseases, and get them you will.
Now we consider a case study. A young lady, unaware,
Contracted cytomeglo virus when she didn't take care.
She did not know she had this disease.
Later she became pregnant with the greatest of ease.
Her son was born with a serious lack.
His mental development would always keep him back.
To hold a job or live on his own, there was no way.

His mom has to care for him for all her days.
When she can no longer do for this man,
The state will provide. At least that's the plan.
The moral is to protect yourself the best you can."

14. Runaway

I got all my money, including what was in the bank.
Lois drove me to the bus station. I'll write to say thanks.
My damn folks were always telling me what to do.
I had to get away. They stifle me, those two.
Don't do this. Don't do that. Stay away from Todd.
I'm old enough to make my own decisions by God.
Now I'll find a job and get my own place.
The city is where it's happening. I'll like the fast pace.
I'll miss some of my friends, but I won't miss home.
Time to get on with my life. There'll be room to roam.
I've seen on TV what city life is about.
There's clubs and bars. You can find guys and make out.
Maybe I'll hook up with some others from out of town.
We can rent a place. It will be our very own.
I'm not sure where I can work or what I'll do.
This is the land of opportunity. I hope that's true.
The bus is coming in. Well here goes.
"Hello young lady. You're new in town. It shows.
My group "Christ for Youth" helps kids find their way.
We have a nice dormitory where you can stay.
We'll help you get a job. What do you say?"
To a sensible adult, this seems pretty shady,
But not to a scared, naive young lady.

15. Tough Love

I loved my son dearly and tried my best
To prepare him for the future when he flew the nest.
A father's duty is to help a boy become a man,
To accept responsibility and to do the best he can.
I told Rob about the dangers of tobacco, drugs and booze,
With familiar examples of how they are abused.
That's why I was so surprised when we found out
Rob was using stuff. By his actions there was no doubt.
We talked to him and asked a teacher to do the same.
He brushed off our concerns. It was a kind of game.
Then it became serious. He started skipping school.
He stopped doing his work and thought he was cool.
Rob quit the band and tennis and dropped a course.
This was bad, but it was about to get worse.
Money started to go missing, then my credit card.
The wife's jewelry disappeared. We should have been on guard.
When we confronted him, Rob just ignored what we said.
What could we do? A counselor proposed what we'd dread.
Have him arrested and then committed for observation.
This would only last a few days, not a salvation.
We didn't do what the counselor suggested we do.
Then things got worse. My worries grew and grew.
He hit his bother and sisters and then my wife.
Everyone was afraid, each afraid for his life.
Then, "Rob get out of the house. You must stay away."
"What are you gonna do, call the cops? That'll be the day."
"Yes, I will if I must. Now take your stuff and get out.
I have to protect the rest of my family," I'd shout.
This was the hardest thing I've done my whole life long.
I know tough love could work, or maybe go wrong.

How will he survive? It's a cruel world out there.
Maybe he'll get help from someone who cares.
I know he'll only be cured after bottom's been hit.
No one else can cure him even bit by bit.

"Sir, I have some bad news I must relate.
Your son Rob has died. This I really hate.
It looks like he O.D.'d. They'll know in a day or two.
He had a note, "I'm sorry, Dad. You did what you had to do.""

16. Never Worked

"I don't understand. You mean your son never had a job?"
"Never, I didn't want him to associate with all those slobs.
If he worked in a restaurant or some retail store,
Or mowed lawns, he might think there's no more.
Since they don't give teenagers leadership positions,
I rather he not work under any lesser conditions.
Of course, he's gone to camp, volunteered here and there,
Taken a few extra courses, these chosen with care.
By the time he's finished college, he should be all set
To step into a good position. I have no regrets."
That poor kid. Life is going to kick his butt.
Will he know how to ask for a job or what?
Maybe he's learning all the theory, but it can't take the place
Of experience, working with people face to face.
He should know he'll have to show up each day.
Though he'd like to sleep late or just stay away.
He doesn't know he has to get along with others,
And do those jobs he'd rather not if he had his druthers.
He'll be expected to work for a full year

Before taking vacation, the poor dear.
Unfortunately, he'll find the world has gotten along
Without this superior young man who was raised wrong.
If I were to hire a youngster and had a choice of two,
I'd definitely pick one who worked hard coming through.
Sweating with the common folks is what you should do.

17. Too Many Hits

"Oh, oh, oh, ah, ah, ah, da, da, Dad?"
"What is it son? It's all just so sad.
Do you want a drink, maybe a bite to eat?
How about some potato, veggies or a piece of meat.
When you played, you were a solid 250 pounds.
You're a shadow of yourself. This disease grinds you down.
You could eat like a horse. You were never fat.
Now the muscle is gone. You're like a drowned rat.
Oh, I know we can't go back. I wish we could.
You were only six. My pushing you was no good.
I know football has been your life all this time.
Now I hate the game. What it does is a crime.
You get repeated concussions. Your brain takes each blow.
There's cumulative damage, but how they don't know.
They even have a name. For us it's CTE.
The old time boxers' punch drunk fits it to a tee.
They told us helmets would protect your brain.
Not to worry, there's just a little pain.
Now I'll take care of you for the rest of your life.
I can't blame her at all when you divorced your wife.
She didn't sign on for a sick old man.
Taking care of your kids, she does the best she can.

Now it's time to get my guy up to bed.
I'll care for you. Believe what I said.
We can pray, toward a cure we'll be led."

18. Early Heart Attack

The young man attended because of his heart attack.
The rehab program was meant to bring health back.
You were to learn what you could do.
There were rules to live by. It was up to you.
We were the half who survived our first event.
To this rehab group we all were sent.
We heard talks by experts and learned the exercise drill
It was necessary to make changes if you had the will.
But this young man was mad as can be.
He thought, "Why is my body betraying me?"
He had the attitude, "I've always done as I wished to do.
I'm not going to change. I won't do anything new."
All of us older survivors decided to go along with the plan.
Life was too sweet for each woman and man.
We joined what was called the maintenance group.
We often talked to the new ones and gave them the scoop.
The young man came back. He was lucky twice.
His attitude changed. To his body he would be nice.
Ignore the advice, then you pay the price.

19. Aspbergers

When he was a kid, Peter always held back.
Other kids gave up. There was something he lacked.
He wouldn't participate, like he'd rather be alone.
Some solitude is all right, maybe more so when
you're grown.

When you play with other kids, you learn
Some social skills, like waiting to take your turn,
What's acceptable in situations and what is not,
How to stand up for yourself in a tricky spot.
Peter grew up and flunked out of college.
He couldn't ask for help to gain the knowledge.
He tried to get close to a gal. She rejected him.
Peter never tried again even on a whim.
He had no people skills his whole life long.
Some call it shyness. It was more. He never belonged.
Now we label it, Aspberger's disease by name.
It's just in time for the result of electronic games.
Too many modern kids, especially the boys,
Are becoming addicted to these devilish toys.
They don't interact with people. Potential friends say
what's the use.
Are they doomed to the lonely life of a recluse?

20. I Can Do It Myself

Infants start out with the easy words you see.
Mama and dada are encouraged with parental glee.
They learn the names of toys and food.
Repeating after Mom if they're in the mood.
Then comes, "I can do it myself" when they grow a bit,
Even when frustration gives them a fit.
"I can dress myself, socks, shirts and pants."
Then, "I can tie my shoes. See me dance."
Sometime early in school, "I can read. I can read."
They have that drive. They want to succeed.
Kids seem anxious to grow up too fast.
When they can drive, "I'm an adult at last."

They look forward to college, life on their own.
You hope with this freedom their health isn't blown.
Then comes the apartment, the sought for job.
"I can do it myself," a status no one can rob.
Later comes family, responsibility without end.
There is no question, for themselves they can fend.
With age sometimes they give up a chore.
Of lawn mowing and snow shoveling they want no more.
Maybe it's infirmities that the old start to feel.
They forget, "I can do it myself" once said with zeal.
Soon they will reach the point as they age,
"Can someone take care of me," defines this stage.
Personally, I plan to fight this with rage.

21. Blameless

"I want to know who did it. Who's to blame?"
In too many families this is their game.
If a kid breaks a vase, he feels bad enough.
No need to rant and rave or huff and puff.
The vase is gone. Assessing blame won't bring it back.
Besides to a child, your anger is an attack.
Better to get the kids together and explain
Why they should be careful. You all can gain.
No punishment is warranted especially if there was no intent.
A peaceful conversation should deliver what's meant.
Better this than a kid doing something bad on the sly,
To avoid punishment, he will keep quiet or lie.
Maybe in his chagrin, he'll run from the scene.
A friend could die, and there's no chance to intervene.
I'm reminded of two boys who were playing with fire.
It started to spread. The results could be dire.

They ran to our house. The fire engines were called out.
We said, "You did the right thing. There is no doubt.
Because of this, we won't tell a soul.
This will be our secret never to be told."
These boys knew what they had done was bad,
No need for them to be punished, no need to be mad.

Chapter 3

Stuff happens. No one's at fault. It's fate.
You just have too much piled on your plate.

1. Hearing

The married couple were both deaf, so I've heard.
It's the way they were born. They couldn't be cured.
They didn't miss sound. That's the way it always was.
Their life required adjustments. Often a handicap does.
They were blessed with a child, and as you'd expect,
He also was deaf. This was a genetic defect.
Modern medicine makes advances over the years.
The doctor told the couple, "We can help your son hear."
With little thought the deaf couple replied, "He's okay.
There's no need. We're not handicapped in any way."
"It's such a shame. He'll never hear the spoken word.
He won't hear a hawk's whistle or the song of a bird.
No Beethoven symphonies, no music, not even rap.
No kitten's meow, no cow's moo, no thunderclap.
When he's out walking, he won't hear the cars.
It's a safety issue. I think you're going too far.
No soft whisper of what young couples like to hear.
When it's quiet and they're alone, "I love you dear."
No telephone, no doorbell, and no phonograph.
But saddest of all, he'll never hear a baby's laugh.
Please think about it. We can help your son.
It will be a wonder for him, a new life begun."

2. Sight

"Let me take your hand, so you won't fall."
"Could you describe what you see? Tell me all."
How can I describe? I know no detail is too small.
The blind man is aware of nothing from wall to wall.
I do my best. I realize how much there's to see.
Most I don't even think about normally.
How do you describe colors from red to blue,
Much less a rainbow or a sunset? I haven't a clue.
Something like the Grand Canyon, no words will do
If I say awesome, does it mean the same as to me and you?
Confucius said, "A picture is worth a thousand words."
I could never be that complete, you can be assured.
This poor man will never know great works of art.
Nature's beauty will always be something apart.
Will he know a baby's smile? Does the word radiant fit?
I know beauty can't be defined. You know it when you see it.
All these things just can't be described to him.
Maybe my enthusiasm will be enough with vigor and vim.
Thank you God. Not being able to read would be a blow.
There is so much more. I appreciate it so.
If I were blinded, the memories would have to suffice I know.

3. Losing a Daughter

Our lovely daughter had rarely been sick in her life.
She called home from college and talked to my wife.
Her gut felt bad, now for several days.
It wasn't associated in other ways
With stuff you'd expect, like food poisoning or flu.
We went to pick her up like concerned parents do.
She immediately had complete medical exams.

They kept doing tests, MRIs and CAT scans.
Finally, the doctor appeared with the worst.
Our daughter with fast spreading cancer was cursed.
They found it in several places, already stage four.
Radiation and chemo were recommended. They couldn't do more.
We were devastated. Why was our daughter picked by fate?
I tried to be strong for my kids and my mate.
When our daughter died, I cried with the rest.
I know for nineteen years, we all had been blessed.
But I will never feel other than the loss we had.
There are no words that will ever make us feel less bad.
More than I can count have said, "I don't know what to say."
Only, "I'm so sorry," will do. You can't dry our tears away.

4. Just Hold Me Mom

My poor baby. Why is she so sick?
Of all people to choose, the fates had to pick.
For those who abuse themselves I can't feel sorry.
When you're old, you die of something. That's the story.
The young shouldn't die with a whole life to live.
She was so happy and gay with so much to give.
This fast moving cancer is a terrible thing.
Barely two weeks ago she could dance and sing.
Now here she lies. The doctors don't have a clue.
The inevitable will happen no matter what they do.
Ah, she's waking up. She looks so beat.
"Maybe you'd like a drink or a bite to eat."
"No, Mom, I can't. Just hold me."
When you have to go, maybe that's how it should be.
Mom who gave you life holding you when your soul goes free.

5. Recent Loss

Oh, God, what a time to lose my great big man.
I'll do my best to take his place if I can.
On the outside he was strong, a go get 'em type.
Who could believe all the heart attack hype?
Thinking back, there were too many "overs" in his life.
I could have helped him. Would I be an overbearing wife?
Cut down on fats and carbs. Exercise some more.
Reduce stress. With his job that was at its core.
Opposed to our well being, the fates did him in.
Maybe it was just the probability wheel spin.
We're almost alone in this world, the three kids and me.
My parents are gone. My brother has his own family.
I think the two older ones in time will be okay,
Though I know they'll miss him each and every day.
Then there's little Ted, just twelve years of age.
Can we help him to grieve? I know he'll have rage.
It's always hard for a son to lose his dad.
The worst is for a preteen. He won't understand. He'll
just be mad.
Damn you, we had a deal you and I.
We promised forever. Why did you have to die?
Sorry, my love. All I can do now is cry.

6. Where's Daddy

"Where's my Daddy? They say that he died.
What does that mean? When I heard it I cried.
Nonnie said he went to heaven to be with God.
God's supposed to be nice. Taking Dad's pretty odd.
He's supposed to stay here at home with me.
Not go off someplace where no one can see.

I looked in my closet and drawers, but he wasn't there.
I looked in the basement. I checked everywhere.
Maybe he got arrested, and they took him away.
That would be a big mistake. He'll be home today.
Maybe he got a job in some far away town.
He'll send a letter and write everything down.
Wherever you are, I don't want you to go.
Daddy, please come home. I miss you so."

7. Spinabifida

"Ah, my beautiful son, we had waited a while for you.
The doctors said you weren't right. They told us what to do.
We should put you in a hospital run by the state.
They would take care of you, but it wouldn't be so great.
We could visit though you would never know.
It's said, God gives us what we can handle. We made it so.
Your Mom and I decided what we'd do.
We'd take care of you, to thine only family be true.
There was no treatment back then for your little brain.
Spinal fluid accumulated with no way to drain.
Your mental and physical age stopped. That was the fear.
You have been a perpetual infant all these years.
This is not the way that life should be,
But we love you so much, Mother and me.
You learned to say Mama and Dada too.
Your recognition smile is the very best you do.
Now it's the time and you're gone. It's God's will.
After seventeen years of infancy, we love you still.

8. Downs

Sometimes I wish I didn't listen to others.
I didn't want that ultrasound though urged by my mother.
My baby may have Downs, the doctor said.
The amniotic fluid test is what I really dread.
There's some danger, but it's a definitive report.
If he has Downs syndrome, they'll expect me to abort.
Well, that's something I'm not going to do.
To our principles, both John and I will be true.
So I'm having no more tests. What will be, will be.
When our son is born, then we will see.
If he has Downs, we'll love him like all is okay,
We'll teach him and help him along life's way.
This will be a lifetime commitment for sure.
Just like every kid, we help make their lives secure.

9. SIDS

Mom: "That bastard, he said my baby had the flu.
I'm his Mom. It was not something like that I knew.
The Doc said, "He'd be better maybe in a day.
Don't worry." Then he sent us on our way.
We changed him, fed him, and put him to bed.
I checked him later, and I found him dead.
Sudden, Infant, Death, Syndrome or SIDS is its name.
A name should help us cope? The doctor's to blame.
I'll sue him for every penny he's got.
I want to get his attention. In hell he should rot."

MD, "How can I explain to them this terrible curse?
Of all calamities this is about the worst.
Nobody can predict who SIDS will hit.

We don't understand it even a small bit.
I know I'll feel sorry for the rest of my days,
Though I have no guilt in any way."

As time passed she was blessed with girls and boys,
None of them replaced her great loss of joy.

10. Chance

Tom was a bachelor. He felt his chances were slim,
Since no woman would want the likes of him.
He talked with a slight lisp due to a hare lip scar.
Everyone who knew him felt that he was a star.
He took it upon himself to help his own,
His poor sister who was raising two boys all alone.
He was a father to them though the age difference was small.
Maybe older brother, he was more accurate to call.
When a coach was needed for the little league team,
Tom volunteered. He was more adept than he seemed.
He was a leader with cubs and later boy scouts.
Tom was the type who always helped out.
He told the boys they should stay in school.
Working hard at whatever you do should be the rule.
The two brothers grew up to be upstanding men.
Not exceptional but better than they could have been.
Tom worked hard. He was honest and good,
But chance had it in for him. Who'd expect it would?
It was Saturday morning with low traffic flow.
He was on a divided highway when fate gave its blow.
A car jumped the center barrier. It landed on Tom's hood.
He died instantly. Why him, Lord? Why take the good?
In a case like this there is no why.
Pure chance caused Tom to die.

11. Trip Home

"We've got a three day weekend. Gotta go.
Enough of this place, but there's a forecast of snow.
I need to study. The others don't seem to care.
They want to BS, and parties are everywhere.
I'll surprise my folks since I'm not expected.
I should like school, but sometimes I feel dejected.
For too many kids this is not their first choice.
Their folks said Ivy League in a loud clear voice.
They feel like failures and come to me.
My shoulders aren't broad enough you'll agree.
So I have to get home and study all I can.
Failing a course is not part of my plan."

"I wish this damn snow would slow down.
I should have left earlier to get out of town.
This is an interstate. Where's all the cars?
My headlights don't help. I can't see too far.
Oh, hell, I'm going off the road.
The cars rolling. Oh, please don't explode."

Announcement: An auto accident on 89 killed Kelly, Beth.
She apparently was unconscious and froze to death.

11. Triple Threat

Carl was a natural athlete you could say.
Kids like him don't come along every day.
In high school students and parents thought he was blest.
He played football and baseball, but at hockey he was best.
On Saturday afternoon people gathered for the game.
Even in the northeast, football tends to inflame.
It's kids playing a game, but we all want to win.

So we cheer and whistle and create a din.
Carl was a running back. He carried the ball.
Passing was mediocre, so he often got the call.
He ran around the end, just a normal running play.
Carl was tackled. Nothing unusual you could say.
The cheering stopped. Coach ran onto the field.
Players gathered around. Some of them kneeled.
Carl was conscious. We could see him move his feet.
Thank God not a spinal injury that no one could treat.
He couldn't walk. They brought a stretcher out.
A bad leg injury, ankle or knee no doubt.
Later when the news came out from his sister Meg,
We found Carl had shattered his lower leg.
He should never skate again his doctor said.
Maybe baseball would be his true calling instead.
On playing college hockey, Carl had his sights set.
Coaches figured going on to the pros was a sure bet.
The big dream wouldn't happen. All was changed.
When an ordinary play was the reason, it's strange.
If you hit life's high point as a teen,
Do you think, "What can the rest of life mean?"
I hope you can say, "I look forward to all the rest.
Of life's adventures, what's coming is still the best."

13. Bipolar

Who knows why a person winds up as she does.
Oldest child? Maybe it was just the way she was.
Her Dad was a real cold fish, a rather rigid guy
Who made life hard for Alma. Maybe that's why.
To follow her Mom's path, she wasn't adverse.
When she finished high school, she became a nurse.

She wanted distance from home, so she joined the Air Force.
Nurses were commissioned second lieutenants of course.
This gave Alma a home and a good income too.
She was stationed out west where everything was new.
That's when her bipolar disease loomed large,
And the Air Force gave her a medical discharge.
She had served only six months, but that was enough.
Alma was a veteran though she didn't have the right stuff.
She met a guy, got married, had a baby girl,
Then quickly got divorced in a bipolar whirl.
Bipolar is the new name for manic depression,
Where you move from heights to depths in rapid succession.
Her life was hard, moving from job to job.
Her daughter suffered, and her youth was robbed.
It was difficult to like Alma due to her ways.
Depression could lay her low for days.
She bothered people talking non-stop in her manic state,
How she would do things that were truly great.
Drugs reduced the swings that she had to bear,
But these made her a non-person, like she wasn't there.
As time flew the daughter grew and had a child.
Her problem was drug addiction. At times she went wild.
And so a mental disease progressed generation to generation.
Maybe the other set of grandparents can stop this aberration.
As for Alma, she moved home after her father died.
She "took care" of her Mom, at least this was tried.
When her Mom died, Alma was left alone.
She needed help. She couldn't make it on her own.
How she did it, nobody seems to know the way.
At a veteran's hospital, Alma got to live out her days,
And even got a military funeral when she passed away.

14. MS

When I started a new job, I met my friend Joe.
He tried to be independent, but his gate was slow.
Joe used a walker which he could fold.
This fit nicely in his car, I was told.
Joe had multiple sclerosis or MS for short.
It affects the nerves and is the progressive sort.
You can think of nerves as electric wires,
Carrying impulses that cause muscles to fire.
If the wires have poor insulation, there are leaks.
The wrong muscles contract for the motion you seek.
We had a car pool. We asked Joe to join us.
Since his home was on the way, there'd be no fuss.
This would be an added benefit for Joe.
We could take his electric cart, the "Amigo."
He was getting worse. Walking was just too hard.
The Amigo allowed him to maintain his self regard.
Joe had that "can do" attitude of the strong.
He kept going with our help for years long.
They had little to alleviate Joe's medical need.
Control tremors by weakening muscles was the creed.
It was hard, but Joe worked 'til incontinence hit.
He was too dignified. For him this was it.
He had the added pain of losing a son.
A stupid motor cycle accident, and he was done.
After a bit Joe needed more medical care.
He was admitted to the VA hospital and died there.
MS is a terrible disease. It doesn't matter what they do.
It robs you of your strength, then your dignity too.
About the cause or a cure, there is no clue.

15. I Don't Have the Right

Since back in the neighborhood, we were best pals.
We attended school together, the inseparable gals.
Even when we wound up in different classes,
We worked together, the studious lasses.
We went to different colleges, of course.
Letters and phone calls were the information source.
We shared our joy when we each fell for a guy.
We were in each others weddings that followed by and by.
We both moved from our childhood haunt.
Never were we too far. The distance didn't daunt.
It was easier for us both with the electronic age.
A quick E-mail kept us up to date at this stage.
We tried to visit each other once a year.
For a weekend or a day, we'd give each other cheer.
There was the inevitable pain. We shared this as well.
It made the hurt more manageable, less of a hell.
As fate would have it, both husbands died.
Each of us held the other as we let go and cried.
Then the worst happened, an accident by car.
I rushed to her side, no distance too far.
My dear friend was conscious but near death.
"Fight for life, fight to your very last breath."
After thought, I said, "I don't really have the right
To tell you how hard that you should fight.
If it hurts too much, it's okay to let go.
I'm your friend for life, if you want it so."
My buddy forever went to join her mate.
I miss her so much with death her fate.

16. Recalcitrant Patient

Sue was old, no need to remind her.
Her body slowed down, that's for sure.
Her legs gave out. She couldn't get up from a seat.
An "electric chair" helped, its boost rather neat.
An elevated toilet seat helped in the john.
Hand holds on the wall could be relied upon.
Her daughter had arrived home to help out.
If truth be told, about motives there was doubt.
Who was taking care of whom in this affair?
All her life the daughter was looking for someone to provide care.
Then as it would happen, Sue suffered from a stroke,
Which left her almost helpless. It was worse than to croak.
What went through her mind? She couldn't speak.
Her legs wouldn't move. Her arms were weak.
Would she spend her last days confined to bed
Unable to communicate? This she surely did dread.
Would she be a burden to her daughter for years?
She couldn't see herself this way through her tears.
Sue was a nurse, so she knew what to do.
She waited for the right time when they changed crews.
Then she pulled out all the tubes and wires,
Hoping no one would notice as she expired.
Damn it, someone saw, and they came on the double.
All was hooked up again, and Sue was in trouble.
She was a recalcitrant patient. They strapped her to the bed.
"Obviously, she doesn't know what she's doing," they said.
The one act she could accomplish, they forbid to her.
She knew exactly what she wanted to occur.
Sometimes God smiles down on us with an unusual gift.
Sue died two days later. Her end was swift.

All sensible people ought to have known Sue's desires.
Few want their last days hooked up to tubes and wires.

17. Language Loss

You talk with each other, no problem here.
Now and then you forget a word, but don't fear.
This just means your brain's slowing down a bit.
No need to worry. Don't have a tizzy fit.
The process is so complicated, how can anyone speak?
Controlling breath, tongue, lips, jaw and even your cheeks.
Your brain controls the whole thing with thousands of words on call.
It's certainly a mystery, how you can do it all.
This one capability separates us from other species.
Like dolphins have sounds, but we can't decipher any of these.
I think language evolved maybe a million years ago.
We had to express difficult ideas I know.
Transferring knowledge to others, especially the young
Was the skill on which our survival hung.
With the growth of knowledge our language kept pace.
Expressions of complicated abstractions are commonplace.
Our brains can understand both the spoken and written word.
We can interpret idioms, sarcasm and dialects heard.
Then as suddenly as a finger's snap,
A tiny blood vessel breaks. It's like a thunderclap.
You lose the ability to express a thought.
All efforts to speak come to naught.
To add to the pain, you can no longer write.
Losing the ability to communicate darkens the night.
How much do you understand? No one knows.
Are you still in there? No intelligence shows.

Can you learn to convey a no or yes?
Blink once or twice. Even this can cause stress.
Though you have that super brain, it's to no avail.
The tiny break means the whole system fails.
You may recover or it's the end of the trail.

18. Why Me?

"I'm a doctor, so I know the rules to live by.
These are publicized, far and wide, low and high.
Everyone should know them unless they don't read.
It's advice that will lengthen life, so take heed.
First of all, make sure you eat the right stuff.
Don't overdo it. Stop when you've had enough.
Exercise regularly. Walking is good all agree.
Between this and diet, keep your weight where it should be.
If you smoke, then stop. It will hasten death.
Clogged lungs mean you can't take a deep breath.
It's very important to cut down on the stress.
It causes high blood pressure. Arteries clog from duress.
The most important is to pick the right parents.
The fact that long life runs in families is apparent.
I've done everything right as it should be,
Then how come this heart attack happened to me?"
You forgot on thing. There's always probability.
Your chances improved. Nothing guarantees the future you see.

19. Alzheimers

The couple had been married for 40 years.
One day came a surprise that brought tears.
Jake, the husband, had a confused look on his face.
He seemed unfamiliar with everything in this place.

His wife had to ask the question. What to do?
Finally, it came out. "You don't know me, do you?"
Jake paused and thought before he said no.
How can a disease deliver such a terrible blow?
Your body may be all right, strong and sound.
When your mind loses all your memories, it astounds.
Aging usually means you forget your keys or a name,
But those lifelong memories are always the same.
How can this disease make you forget your wife,
The closest person to you for most of your life?
Of all the ways for you to decay, I find
The saddest by far is to lose your mind.

20. Allie

Why is it we love our animals so much?
We pet them, scratch them, and hug them and such.
Our Allie was a black lab with a tiny bit of white.
She was mild mannered and sweet. She'd never fight.
Other dogs could visit and share her water bowl.
Going out the door, being first was not her goal.
She drew the line at her food bowl of course.
A low throated growl was enough, the law to enforce.
We'd take her for walks never needing a lead.
She would frequently check, our whereabouts she'd heed.
Even on the coolest days, if there was water about,
Allie would swim. She was a water dog no doubt.
When she came out, she'd be cold to the core.
Then she'd race back and forth to warm up more.
The crazy dog routine, we called this one.
Sometimes all the dogs would do it for fun.
One time she panicked when she got water in her nose,

And I jumped in with my shoes and clothes.
Like the other dogs, we loved her so.
Cancer appeared at 16, and so she had to go.
Briefly, at the vet's, she got up to get close to me.
False hope on my part. It wasn't meant to be.
She went peacefully and in the absence of pain.
She joined her predecessors. In our pet cemetery she's lain.
We wish our pets lived longer, but it's not so ordained.

21. Peppi

Our family pet suddenly disappeared one day.
We searched and asked around. Where did she stray?
Someone kidnapped her. We had other evil thoughts.
We'd heard that for medical research dogs were bought.
After a period of mourning we answered an ad.
"Puppies for sale, part German Shepherd," is what they had.
We went and found one female remained.
We'd like to buy this last one we explained.
A young girl owned it along with her Dad.
She wanted to make sure we wouldn't be bad.
We promised we'd take care of her puppy pet.
We'd even keep the name "Peppi," so she needn't fret.
So Peppi came and lived with us and our kids four.
She was smart as can be. You could ask for no more.
I'd whistle when she barked, and she'd come home.
Soon if she barked, she'd come home on her own.
We always let our dogs roam. There was no leash law.
Unfortunately, they'd wander off, freedom's flaw.
Our Peppi had a friend who drew her away,
And resulted in her death. A car hit her that day.
Danger is the risk of freedom you could say.

22. Tornado

"I suppose we should be used to the siren's alarm.
The "powers that be" want to keep us from harm.
The damn thing went off yesterday, then it turned clear.
No big storm came by, and we had nothing to fear.
We're in the region the weathermen call tornado alley.
We had another alarm, too many to tally.
I heard a roaring sound coming from the west.
I went to take a look, to do this seemed best.
The sky darkened, then by God there was a funnel cloud.
I yelled, "Quick, kids, into the bathroom. It's so loud.
Lie down in the tub. That should protect you."
With no basement, what else could we do?
The sound engulfed us like 100 railroad trains.
The house started shaking. Could it take the strain?
Windows were shattering. The roof ripped off.
I remember seeing all the debris aloft.
The kids were petrified, scared beyond belief.
They hugged the tub praying for relief.
To us it was eternity, but took 30 seconds to go by.
At that time we thought we would die.
When we got up, the house walls were all gone.
Wood and assorted junk covered the lawn.
We all had some bleeding with scratches and welts.
Nobody was aware of when these were dealt.
We survived though I don't understand how.
Seeing all the destruction, it seems unbelievable now."
These people lived through a tornado of force five.
With wind so high, speed indicators never survive.
In the city of Joplin almost 7000 homes were lost,
While only 160 people was the human cost.

Seeing the devastation, one can only wonder why.
Maybe a Devine hand limited the number who died.
With climate change will it get worse as time goes by?

23. To the Rescue

I heard the weather report and knew I must go.
My wife will call my job sites, so they'll know.
I threw my chain saw and some tools in the back.
The rest is filled with water and junk food snacks.
Seeing the destruction, there's too much for the rescue crews.
Maybe volunteers can help with all there's to do.
I'm coming up on the town. I'll ask this cop.
"Turn around, we want no rubber neckers to stop."
"I came to help. I have food, water, stuff like that."
"Okay. Go ask that guy with the yellow hard hat."
"We're glad for all the help we can get.
We have to work fast. Some are still alive yet.
Go down six blocks and work back this way.
Look for movement. Listen to what someone might say.
Here are flags, You'll need both black and red.
Red's for a live one you can't get to. The black's for the dead."
No road signs. Here's six blocks. Oh, no search needed here.
An old woman, no pulse, she's cold poor dear.
I'll plant a black flag, but maybe there are more.
What's his? A cute little dog hiding under a door.
Come here boy. What are you trying to tell me?
Let me follow you. Someone's under that debris.
Oh my Lord, a little girl. She's not hurt bad.
She's breathing okay. Where's her mom and dad?

Making sure her back was okay (she could wiggle her toes),
I got her to the first aid station tent, easy as she goes.
I checked later, and her worried parents were found.
The whirlwind blew her hundreds of feet across the ground.
Her family had no dog. I checked at the pound.
I looked everywhere for the dog but with no success.
If he had no family, then ours would be blessed.
Guardian angels can take many guises I guess.

24. Tornado Needs

"I can't help in a tornado disaster. What do I know?"
There's more than you can imagine if you give it a go.
First, think of rescue crews, those who save the lives.
For this you need a strong back, no surprise.
Someone pulled from the wreckage has transportation needs,
Including driving or stretcher bearing with reasonable speed.
To safeguard the rescuers, electricians need to cut power.
You don't want people electrocuted with a spark shower.
Plumbers are needed where houses are served with gas.
It would be unfortunate to die in a blast.
The water should be turned off to each house too.
Surviving the wind, then drowning in the basement won't do.
Survivors and rescuers require water and food.
Both are needed no matter your mood.
Maybe you can unfold cots and put up tents.
Too many there, have no shelter, women or gents.
Some need clothes replacing, those blown off their backs.
Cool weather doesn't stop tornados in their tracks.
Medical personnel are needed, could you assist?
In the worst case, mortuary services join the list.

The whirlwind destroys street signs on its day,
These need painting on pavement to find your way.
Neighborhoods may be unrecognizable, even your own block,
Where your house used to be, you have to take stock.
Maybe you can help people search their own space,
For important papers, photos, durable items you shouldn't
need to replace.
Every person whose house has been destroyed
Will welcome your help. They'll be overjoyed.
Maybe their spirits by you will be buoyed.
For the victims in the worst type tornado path,
It's about the most destructive of nature's wrath,
Including earthquakes, flood, hurricane and fire.
It's a true holocaust with results most dire.

25. The "No" Problem

"Dear God, thank you for saving our family whole.
We'll be eternally grateful both heart and soul.
But we've got some real problems I call the "nos."
We have no house. It received one heck of a blow.
The tornado smashed everything. We have no cars.
We have no stuff. It's scattered over many yards.
I wish all the photographs weren't lost,
Since they're not replaceable. They're beyond cost.
I was a manager, but now there's no store.
One thing really bothers me. Are "we" no more?
We have no documents that show we exist.
Our drivers licenses and credit cards are on that list.
Pass books, check books, birth certificates, and passports too.
Our insurance papers went when the wind blew.
Even my cell phone disappeared with my wallet.

We're okay but a true disaster is what I'd call it.
My brother and sister as well as my wife's
Are barely getting by in their own personal lives.
Our parents are pretty old and are just squeaking by.
None can help. Anyway, we can't travel by car nor can we fly.
Today we'll be starting from scratch, but then
We have each other. We will survive. Amen."
"I've seen you at the shelter. You're a good man.
My wife and I have a big house. Here's the plan.
We'll put you up 'til you're back on your feet.
Please don't try to pay us. This will be our treat.
Just promise to pass it on to someone you meet.

Chapter 4

The war is over, have we won?
Sorry your personal battle has just begun.

1. Mistakes Happen

The Thunderbolt was the heaviest fighter in the war,
Very fast when diving, but the pilots wanted more.
Al would like it more maneuverable, like now.
The Hun was on his tail. Escape? No how.
"I'm too low to bail. The engines sputtering away.
There's a field. Maybe I'll make it. I can only pray."
Al made his crash landing, wounded but alive.
He opened the canopy and took a dive.
As he limped away, his plane burst into flame.
"I have to get to the woods. I wish I wasn't lame."
His fellow pilots spotted the flaming wreck.
"Did anyone see a chute? I'll make a quick check.
I think no one could make it out of that fire.
We salute you Al in that funeral pyre."
The pilots reported Al's death back at their base.
In this instance the wheels turned with untoward haste.
Within days Gloria, Al's lovely 20 year old wife
Got the notifying telegram about Al's loss of life.
Of what happened above, Al was unaware.
The plane was a beacon. He had to get away from there.
He came to a country road. There was a boy on a bike.
"Sorry, Junge, but I need that. You'll have to hike."

We weren't supposed to steal. It was the Army's rule.
Sometimes survival requires we be mildly cruel.
Al peddled west 'til he blew a tire.
Then he had to walk though his leg felt on fire.
He walked and hid, finding a brook for a drink.
His survival rations gave out. His spirits didn't sink.
With prayers, skill and luck, Al made it back to our side.
"I have no desire to be a POW," he cried.
About the telegram home*, Al finally found out.
He raised all kinds of hell, being alive there was no doubt.
Finally, poor Gloria after a month of hell,
Found her beloved Al was alive and well.
Al recovered from his wounds and returned to the States.
Prayer and perseverance determined his fate,
The young couple prospered man and wife.
They raised five kids and had a great life.
*Normally, KIA telegrams require proof that's real,
Otherwise, Missing in Action somewhat lessens a wife's ordeal.

2. The Dream

"You're groaning. Wake up! Wake up Dad!"
"It's my usual dream. The one I've always had.
It's been the same for the last fifty years."
"Maybe if you tell me, it'll stop right here."
"No one has ever heard it, ever. I guess you're right.
Now I'm dying, maybe I can clear away my blight.
It's like it was yesterday, the images so clear.
We're going ashore. The beach is near.
Running engines and explosions make a deafening noise.
We're jumping from the boat, a bunch of teenage boys.
Bullets are splashing around us. The water's red.

I smell explosives and the spilled guts of the dead.
I'm gripped by unbelievable fear. I freeze.
My buddy Jim tries to drag me in from the seas.
Then he gets it. Jim's dead instead of me.
I've had this guilt. Why can't I be free?"
"Dad, just thank God. It wasn't time for you.
Think of Mom, your kids, and grand kids too.
We wouldn't be here. This is what was meant to be."
"I still have the guilt. Maybe God can forgive me.
I can rest easier now, you know.
Surviving the war was God's will. That softens the blow."

3. The Second Wave

We were not to hit the beach until nine.
We're going in early. Is that a good sign?
It seems a bit more quiet. The noise has dropped.
Maybe the action has slowed or stopped,
Or else the first wave are all wounded or dead.
I'm not sure what the quiet means up ahead.
Will we wade ashore with no danger there,
Or will it be a meat grinder, we can't bear?
Stop thinking, stop thinking, just do as you're told.
Whatever we face, be aggressive and bold.
I'll think about something else, where the stuff is in my pack,
About home and my family, how it will be when I get back.
I'll say a little prayer. It's selfish what I say,
But I hope the first wave all survived, I pray.
Give us strength, Lord, they're dropping the ramp.
Here goes. The first thing, we're going to get damp.
I've made it this far. Now if all goes well,
Maybe luck will be with us, and we won't enter hell.

4. The Movie House

This incident happened in World War II, I kid you not.
It was in a southern state and the weather was hot.
The prison camp was all German. They had been good.
The commander said he'd reward them if he could.
They took a bus load to a movie in the nearby town.
We are nice. Everywhere else POWs are kept down.
Meanwhile, a group of black GIs got a pass from base.
They decided to see a movie at the same place.
At the time there was a strict racial separation.
The black soldiers had their seating location.
How about the POWs, with the whites, no need to guess.
What were those GIs fighting for, to safeguard this mess?

5. Farm Help

The POW camp was not far from the farms.
Most sons had volunteered and were under arms.
The farmers needed labor. Using POWs made sense.
Would this work? Maybe the situation would be too tense.
The guards talked to the POWs. They needed to work.
Hanging around with nothing to do, they'd go berserk.
They were all healthy. Of that we made sure.
We were confident they'd behave. We'd be secure.
The farmer and his wife only needed one hand.
They got young Otto who had lived on the land.
This worked out quite well for all concerned.
The farmer even insisted Otto keep money he earned.
They taught him English. Mixing languages was fun.
He ate at their table and was treated like a son.
The farmer gave Otto books to help him learn.

Finally, Otto asked, "You're so nice. I'd expect you to be stern."

The farmer explained, "I think your folks worry about you.

We're the same inside. I really think this is true.

If they had the chance, they'd do as we do."

About the farmer's son's death, Otto never knew.

6. Stalag Education

"The guys elected me leader. I answered the call.

It's one time we haven't followed military protocol.

The Huns separate their prisoners. We don't know what for.

We're all non-coms in the Army Air Corps.

I think they felt with no officers in charge,

We'd be easier to manage, each being just a sarge.

They're not aware that when the need is there,

We will step forward and take the leadership chair.

Early on we decided to stick together like glue.

Teamwork means we and us, not me and you.

We meet together regularly. Every man gets a say.

We will practice only equality every day.

Anyone who gets special treatment from the guards

Is shunned by the rest of us afterwards.

We need secrecy when planning and working for an escape.

Maybe we'll practice some deception leaving them agape.

Even when some of us make it out of here,

The need to keep busy is quite clear.

One of the men noticed some of us can't read,

So we started a school to fill the need.

We found we have enough expertise to teach.

More courses were developed that were in our reach.

You have to be inventive with few books or aids.

Several guys teaching together helps us make the grade.
When we get home after this war is done,
Quite a few will go back to school. Of these I'll be one."
The POW leader* did go to school after the war.
He became a teacher to help kids that need more.
*A colleague taught ROTC.

7. The POW Returns

It's been a few years since I stayed at the farm.
The old couple was so nice. Hope they came to no harm.
We were POWs. The Wehrmacht told us so many lies.
When we were sent home, we should sever all ties.
The Americans were not our friends. We should never write.
Well I remembered the address. They knew I might.
I heard about POWs traveling back to the USA,
To relive that POW life of a bygone day.
We were treated well, and the men's spirits were high.
We secretly were so happy the war passed us by.
A few felt shame that we were prisoners of war.
It was better to die for the Fuhrer? What for?
Thinking back, POW time was the best experience of my youth.
I came back to see why this was the truth.
There's the farm. I hope they're still there.
Maybe they won't remember me or won't care.
They're answering the door. What will be, will be.
"My God, it's Otto. Bessie, come see, come see."
As he hoped, he was welcomed like a long lost son.
To hell with war. Here love has won.

8. World War II POW

After World War II, too many thought POWs were a disgrace.
When you were taken prisoner, it was a loss of face.
Many, quick to judge, had never faced enemy fire.
The question is, "Will it help our cause if I expire?"
When you're out of ammo and have no means to resist,
Doing so is just suicide, bullet against fist.
So judge not lest you be judged my friend.
Better to live then to meet a meaningless end.
"Hey, young fella, looks like you could use a ride.
I can't see you getting far with those crutches by your side.
What happened? Did you wait at the shelter where they share?
You should have had a dozen offers out there."
"Oh, I got a ride all right. We were talking about the war.
When I told him I was a POW, he told me to open the door.
He didn't want to associate with the likes of me.
No matter that there's nobody around as far as you can see.
I got my wound fair and square. Part of my leg's gone.
I was lucky a German medic came along.
That guy spent the whole war sitting on his butt.
Never been shot at. Probably got a medal for a paper cut.
I did my share, D-Day and eight months at the front.
Now I have to take crap and that kind of stunt."
"I guess not all the pricks were Japs and Huns.
You've got a ride as far as you want, son.
You're about my own boy's age. He didn't come back.
I can accept that now. It was a Kamikaze attack.
To me you're a hero when that uniform you don.
After that it's fate or luck or what path you're on.
You going to the railroad station or the bus?
If there's time, could you share a meal with us?

Maybe we can help you forget that ornery cuss?
Now, you don't worry. It won't be a fuss"
They traded addresses, the old couple and the youth.
A long time friendship followed for the benefit of both.

9. Obit (With an American Flag)

Alfred Curio passed away peacefully on April twenty first.
His parents were Alfredo and Maria of Parkhurst.
Mr. Curio was predeceased by brother Robert and sister Joan.
No surviving relatives are known.
At eighty six he was a long term resident of the VA.
The funeral will be held privately on Saturday.
A memorial service is scheduled at ten on the sixth of May.
Please join us in the VA chapel as we pray.

"Oh, how sad. That's Al from back in school.
He joined the Marines. I said don't be a fool.
I thought he was killed since he never came home.
Has he lived all these years in the hospital alone?
If I only knew, I could have visited him there.
I'll go to the memorial service and say a prayer."

10. Back to Normandy

My wife and I are traveling back while we still can.
I had often wondered if it was a good plan.
That day was the most of a lot of things.
I think most terror is what memory brings.
I had wanted to approach the beach from the sea.
It would be more realistic, but that couldn't be.
I'll look down, and my memory will have to do.
It's early, shortly after day break, and cloudy too.

It's June sixth and as planned, we have a low tide.
My God, we crossed that. The beach is so wide.
We heard the bombers before dawn when out at sea.
They were to crater the beach, but this wouldn't be.
Later we learned all bombs hit miles inland,
So we had no cover when we crossed the sand.
The naval guns started up and had their round.
They had no effect against fortifications on high ground.
When our boats came in and the ramps were dropped,
We jumped and struggled and tried to avoid getting popped.
Bullets were flying all around. Most everyone got hit.
I got a couple of minor wounds. They only hurt a bit.
When I think of all the destruction and death,
I'll wonder how I made it to my very last breath.
After a few hours we gained the high ground.
Then I paused for a minute and looked around.
This beach was covered with debris of every kind.
Dead tanks and smashed landing craft come to mind.
The boats kept coming in with more men and supplies.
Wounded were lying there waiting to say their goodbyes.
Now I look out and think what a beautiful spot.
All the detritus of war is no longer a blot.
Man has recycled some. Nature took care of the rest.
I'm glad I came back. I know my life has been blessed.

11. Going Back

People we've met say going back is what you should do.
You may visit the battlefields but visit cemeteries too.
Here we are. They take good care of the grounds.
The size of this place, it truly astounds.
All the crosses and stars, just so in their lines.

When I think what it means, it blows my mind.
How many lives cut short, they got no chance to live.
All those broken hearts, it was too much to give.
The fathers and brothers, husbands and sons,
Coworkers, classmates or neighbors were the ones.
Maybe if they had lived, they'd had done something great.
Could one of their descendants have altered our fate.
Great or not, everyone should have a go
At living and loving or the possibility of making it so.
Maybe all the leaders should tour a field of the dead,
To get thoughts of warfare out of their heads.
How to save life, they should think of instead.

12. The Guard

Here I am, a former guard and 90 years of age.
Even after all this time, I can understand their rage.
What we did was the worst kind of sin.
That's the main reason for the trouble I'm in.
Other's have said it's what we were ordered to do.
Good soldiers must follow orders, it's true.
But there's more that is never mentioned.
Keeping us there at any cost was their intention.
The Russian front is where I had served my time.
I lost most of my toes in that hellish clime.
I was unfit for duty, but that would change fast.
Refuse an order and in Russia I'd repeat my past.
Also, it was widely known how else we would pay.
Our families would be grabbed and taken away.
I know there is nothing that will absolve my crime.
Still I won't go to jail in my remaining time.

13. What's True

There are collections of oral histories from the men
Who fought in our wars way back when.
These are studied to try to understand what they went through,
And to give history a personal feel and hue.
Of all stressful experiences, combat is about the worst.
Any man who's exposed will consider himself cursed.
What is remembered is determined by the state of mind.
Two guys sharing a foxhole see things differently you'll find.
Your senses are overloaded with sound and sight.
It's too much for some, and they can no longer fight.
Sometimes the fury will so overload the brain,
The soldier can be unaware of serious pain.
As a defense against total mental collapse,
Memories are erased. The brain creates a lapse.
Substitute memories can develop over the years,
And these can be just as realistic and clear.
Historians have to take this into account
When interpreting memories, what do you accept or discount.
Occasionally, a man's recollections are flat out wrong,
Since participating units' rosters show he never belonged.
I would go easy on men who make heroic claims,
Unless seeking public office is their aim.

14. Seeking a Friend

Lately, I've been thinking of the distant past.
I am aging. Why does time travel so fast?
Unbidden, I have thoughts on the years of war.
Most of this I've tried to forget. I wanted no more.
My friend Bob and I had been together and our life was tough,
Basic training, infantry training, pre-invasion stuff.

We went ashore on Normandy, then in a few weeks,
Bob got it at St. Lo where our drive hit its peak.
Last time I saw him, the medics took him away.
He was all bloody. I felt it was his final day.
I got wounded myself, twice in fact.
I was so lucky to have made it back.
After all this time, I wonder if Bob made it.
Did he die that day with too big a hit?
I know the military has records. I'll give it a try.
That would be something if he didn't die.
The internet surely will help. I'll begin there.
All I know is his name and hometown. I have time to spare.

Bob, you have a common name, and that's no longer home.
However, I got your serial number. I can find where you roam.
You survived those wounds, you sun of a gun.
Maybe we can get together and remember the "fun."

Bob's been in this VA hospital in his declining days.
Here's his room, maybe I should go away.
"Hey, Bob, it's been a long time. Remember me?"
"By God, it's Joe. I'm falling apart, but I can still see.
I was with you when I took that shot.
Thought you probably got it too, like as not."
Maybe two old buddies can remember when they were great.
They have this limited time before it's too late.

15. War Friends

In a war being close friends is the normal state.
You share the danger. You share the fate.
Where else do men die without a thought

To protect their buddy as the battle's fought.
Maybe it's training or instinct to expose yourself to fire
While dragging a wounded man to safety. Then you expire.
You may not even know the guy,
Which is true of medics who themselves die.
Sometimes life-long friendships are forged in war.
Survivors have reunions after years pass by the score.
Others want to forget that bond. Remembering is pain.
Too many were lost, severely wounded or slain.
A squad of ten could have 30 or 40 pass through.
Replacements for all those lost members of the crew.
Most true bonds made in war don't last,
Since only one is left to remember the past.

16. Bill's Luck or God's Will

"I was looking through my special drawer
Where I save odds and ends, like stuff from the war.
I came across my St. Christopher's medal from back then.
I told you of its significance when you were about ten.
You may not remember, so I'll retell the story.
We expected a Chinese attack that would get gory.
I wasn't Catholic, but I needed all the help I could get.
I got the medal from our chaplain. It seemed a good bet.
I put it on the dog tag chain around my neck.
The attack began. I spent most of the time on the deck.
We'd each raise up, fire a few rounds, then duck.
The enemy had no time to aim, this providing some luck.
Once I felt a thud, but there wasn't any pain.
I thought no more about it not knowing what I'd gained.
Days later we had showers. Our clothing we changed.
A slug fell out of my shirt. I thought how strange.

Then I noticed the medal with its dent.
Examining my shirt, I saw where the bullet went.
It was aimed at my heart, a death shot.
The medal had slipped over to that very spot.
Was it good luck or God's will? I know no more.
I just know I'll always be thankful I survived the war.
Son, I want you to keep this. Remember the story I've told.
Then pass it on to your son when you get old."

17. Coming Home

"That was quite a flight. I'm as tired as can be.
It's a good thing Al, that soldier, was flying with me.
Getting in and out of the wheelchair, he helped me a lot.
I've still got one good leg, the other's about shot.
Al was traveling on up north, Bangor I guess.
My folks are supposed to pick me up. Maybe traffic's a mess.
I'll wait here. They're sure to spot my wheels.
I've never been like this. Helpless is how it feels.
Well, better a partial cripple than being back in Nam.
When I get my strength back, it's crutches by damn.
Now what's going on? Something else to make my day?
Oh, God, war protesters, and they're coming my way."
"There's one. Dirty baby killer, I spit on you.
Get out of Nam. Here's red paint for what you do."
"Shame on you all. Leave the guy alone.
I may be an old man, but this I won't condone.
Go near him, and you have to go through me.
Get out of here. He's wounded can't you see.
Guess they're going to commit another crime.
Hey. Soldier, I'll stay with you for a time.
Damn hippies are mad at the government about the war.

How does hassling a wounded soldier help on that score?
I'll clean you up a bit. That paint may never come out."
"Thank you sir. If I can say so, you have quite a clout."
"One GI to another, here the outcome was never in doubt."

18. Racial Tolerance

"I want to give you some history to help explain
Why I may haul off and give you some pain.
Back a few years ago, I was damn mean,
Probably the worst sum-bitch you've ever seen.
I used the N word whenever I saw a black.
We'd fight and maybe a few heads we'd crack.
This kept up 'til I joined the Army, Airborne.
The military was integrated, but them I'd still scorn.
There were enough black NCOs to keep me in line
Though I imagine white ones were also so inclined.
Going through basic, one guy I did really hate.
I gave him a hard time. His name was Nate.
We were in the same platoon when we got to Nam.
On one mission, the brass got us in a jam.
They thought they'd spotted a concentration of gooks.
Copters carried us in to take a look.
We were on the ground when all hell broke out.
It's like the Cong knew our plans with no doubt.
We called in the gun ships, artillery too.
I took one in the leg, through and through.
Nate was beside me. He stopped the blood.
He dragged me to the Huey through the mud.
He got me there, and they loaded me aboard.
I looked back and saw Nate, oh my Lord.
He was dead as plain as I could see.

The poor bastard lost his life saving me.
I had some time recuperating for deep thought.
I'll never know the answers that I sought.
I just know I'm going to make it up if I can
By being a completely tolerant kind of man.
That's why I give a warning about what I might do
If I ever hear a racist remark from you.
But then maybe Nate wouldn't want me to."

19. The Best

Gerry joined the Army at 18. What else should he do?
They offered the promise. In retrospect they came through.
But not in what you'd call the expected way.
Gerry was serving in Iraq on that fateful day.
He was driving his Humvee. An explosion took place.
The sergeant who pulled him out said, "Don't touch your face."
He received burns over a quarter of his body in the attack.
He looked in the mirror, and a freak stared back.
He was devastated. This was too big a blow.
Despair, too mild a word, down from that he'd go.
Then as all would hope, a miracle happened due to his mom.
She said a few words. Call it maternal balm.
"Whoever is going to be there in life for you,
Will be there for love, not because of looks." It's true.
Gerry's attitude changed. He became a new man.
The Brooks Army Medical Center helped with his plan.
He had 30 operations over the next three years.
During this time he helped others with hope and cheer.
He joined a group to help veterans in need,
Non-covered medical bills, new houses, other good deeds.
Gerry continues to be a model for burn victims out there.

His encouragement helps their pain to bear.
He's the human face of the thousands of guys
Who have been physically scarred in war, our GIs.
Gerry is among the very best. He gets the prize.

20. Balance

I never thought about the sense of balance before.
You just had it. You didn't fall to the floor.
That is unless you twirled around and around.
Getting dizzy meant you crashed to the ground.
You messed up the tiny accelerometers in your inner ear,
Which has nothing to do with the ability to hear.
When your head moves, they measure the minute force.
Then the brain sends messages to muscles in due course.
If you stand on one foot, you can feel the action.
Your balance is maintained by the muscle reaction.
Why do I think about this sense now?
I lost both my feet. I'll walk again I vow.
I can't picture balancing with no brain control.
They do wondrous things, but they can't make you whole.
I'll get by with crutches, then a cane or two.
Baring a truly great prosthesis, that will have to do.

21. PTSD

What happens to men after they've gone through hell?
Death had been near. Buddies didn't do so well.
The memories will always be in their dreams.
If they're lucky, life will be okay or so it seems.
In the far distant past of World War I,
It was called shell shock 'til that war was done.

Battle fatigue was the chosen name in World War II,
Which hardly describes what the men went through.
We have a tendency in our country to change names
When the meaning with use is not the same.
Post Traumatic Stress Disorder or PTSD
Is the latest moniker for what doctors see.
Any man suffering from this will be depressed.
Most likely his feelings won't be expressed.
He will be quiet and to himself he'll cry.
He can't forget the hell no matter how he tries.
As with most depressed people, no one will know,
And in day-to-day life it will not usually show.
Contrary to what TV programs like to portray,
PTSD people do not randomly hurt or slay.
If life becomes too hard, they'll end their own days.
To stop the anguish, suicide seems the only way.

22. On Returning Home

"My last deployment is over. Thank the Lord.
I've had enough of military life, though I was never bored.
It's not that there was much choice on my part.
My wounds make me unfit though I have the heart.
They always told us we are leaders of men.
I've thought about this relative to where I've been.
Now I'm looking for a job, so what experience applies?
I could be a councilor when someone is hurt or dies.
I could manage a team of security guards.
Maybe the Secret Service should be my reward.
There's one thing where I could do a good job.
That's being a hit man for the boss of the mob.
I should never joke about that sort of stuff.

Leadership in civilian life will be different enough.
I've talked with other ex-military men.
They told me what I should never mention again.
Never talk about wounds or my mental stress.
They've heard too much about guys being a mess.
I'm to make up good stories about where I've been,
No combat, no wounds, no killing of men.
I suffered from a training accident in a car.
That explains my limp and the facial scars.
Why is it we've given our country more than our share?
Yet of ex-military, too many seem to be scared?
I should point out, I'm on their side,
And I will never, ever look for a free ride."

Chapter 5

Sometimes we can suffer from society's rules.
Are things set up by a bunch of fools?

1. No Good Deed Goes Unpunished

Seth had kidney failure. Soon he would die.
They tested relatives, to find a transplant is why.
They determined brother John was a perfect fit.
With no hesitation John said, "I don't mind a bit.
You can use one of mine since I have two.
How soon do we start? Do what you have to do."
The operation went as the doctors planned.
Seth started feeling better. Soon he could stand.
But donor John was feeling kind of low.
His wife visited him, and it was like a blow.
She saw a nurse, "My husband is hot as can be.
He looks pretty bad as anyone can see."
"Oh, don't worry. He's okay. His brother is doing fine."
The wife settled down having heard the medical line.
John didn't improve. His wife asked around.
A busy doctor was the next person she found.
"He's got a fever. His lower back has a rash."
"He's okay. He had major surgery. I have to dash."
Nobody would listen, so she started raising hell.
Finally, they came and found he wasn't doing well.
They had paid no attention, now John was near death.
Naturally, everyone had been concerned with Seth.

The abscess where the kidney was had to be drained.
Antibiotics were administered, but John was pained.
He recovered, but his life was changed forever.
All connections to his occupation, he had to sever.
He was an exterminator in contact with poison each day.
This would kill him is all they could say.
The hospital claimed no fault in any way.
For their carelessness they should pay.
A hospital caused infection gave John that hit.
"No good deed goes unpunished," seems to fit.

2. Trust

Well, here I am. Have to go in the door at the back.
Never go in the front door. It's not for blacks.
They gave me a key. Don't disturb the Misses, that's the rule.
The first thing is get the kids up for school.
She left me a note, what the kids should eat,
What each should wear, check the homework's neat,
Fix Billy-Bob's lunch, money for the other two,
Remind Becka about piano lessons. It's enough to do.
Good thing I love these kids, but I can't treat them like mine.
I expect mine to take care of themselves most of the time.
I put on the coffee. That's all the Mister wants.
He likes to eat down town at one of his haunts.
The Misses will call down later for a bite.
She likes to lie in bed as you'd expect she might.
Got to make sure the kids get out the door.
Then, I clean up the kitchen. My note has more.
Lordy sakes, that women needs a personal aide.
Someone to guide me, stuff to be done or made.
Later I'll have to do laundry, vacuum, and dust.

In the meantime, being quiet is a must.
The ironing will keep me busy 'til I get the call.
Most of the time I can be my own boss and all.
There is one strict rule. They have made it quite clear.
I must never use their bathroom while I'm here.
It's like I have some disease or I'm unclean.
Yet I'm intimate with everything if you know what I mean.
I prepare the food, wash the dishes and clothes,
Take care of the kids more than anyone knows.
Often they treat me bad, sometimes like dirt,
And yet they trust me. Do they know how it hurts?
What a good person I am, maybe they'll never know,
But both God and I know that this is so.
This is my lot in life 'til it's time to go.

3. Tolerance

We get pressured into being tolerant toward every kind.
If you don't think too much, this seems fine.
I certainly want to be tolerant of every race.
For all ethnic groups, in our country there is a place.
Then I start to wonder about all beliefs.
The practice of human sacrifice, oh no, good grief.
Well, how about sacrificing animals, is it okay?
I think animal rights groups would have a say.
Should I tolerate groups like the Nazis of World War II?
They believed in killing off people, especially the Jews.
Our church at one time wanted to make it very clear,
That independent of sexual orientation, "You're welcome here."
Well, gays are okay. How about predatory types?
Do we want pedophiles and others of that stripe?

There are groups that think you should publicly stone
A young rape victim who has no sin to atone.
Should we tolerate people who think it's okay to steal,
Or cheat, lie, or bully? How do they make you feel?
Should you be tolerant of those who say you're an infidel,
And do their best to send you to hell.
I can be compassionate to many out there.
Just don't expect tolerance of what I can't bear
We should use our heads and judge with care.

4. Big Questions

The old people gathered for discussions each week.
They talked about current events. Understanding they'd seek.
The moderator asked a series of questions to them.
Some they could answer. For others they'd haw and hem.
What religion has a billion followers or more?
Oh, that's easy. There's at least two on that score.
Where are religious fanatics fighting neighbors on every side?
Could we have a hint? Do you mean world wide?
Who doesn't mind bombing anyone, friend or foe?
We can think of several. These are countries we know.
Who never sends aid for their fellow man?
When natural disaster strikes, for help there's no plan.
Who never says thanks when receiving our aid?
Well, that could be anyone. Many make the grade.
Who treats half their people like slaves or worse?
That's a given. For that they should be cursed.
Finally, about this religion can anything good be said?
After thought, they pray five times a day I've read.
Maybe they pray that all infidels be struck dead.

5. Homeless

"I lost my job, no fault of my own.
The factory shut down. Now I feel all alone.
The wife took the kids. They fled to her kin.
She didn't want to share the trouble I'm in.
Unemployment comp, helped us, but just for awhile.
I sent most of it to the wife. That's my style.
The bank foreclosed on the house, those bums.
I sold what was left here, at least some.
Furniture and all were real bargains I think,
But nobody has any money, which really stinks.
The house has to be clear, so the sheriff came by.
They piled it all on the curb. See the grown man cry.
I hope they call the Salvation Army today.
It's silly for all my stuff to be just thrown away.
I packed some clothes, some food and stuff,
Odds and ends that could be useful enough.
My backpack and a full gym bag are all I have left.
With these few possessions, I have to worry about theft.
Now what happens? Where do I sleep? Where do I go?
Where will my next meal come from? I just don't know.
I can't help wishing this was back in the depression.
Hobos didn't have it so bad. That's my impression.
They were often given food by farmers' wives.
Then they did some work to help themselves survive.
Riding the rails, they could travel around.
They didn't want to overstay in any one town.
Now knock on any door and here's the deal,
You'll be a guest in jail, but then maybe there's a meal.
The cops will give you a ride to the town line.
Relatively speaking on my trek I'm doing fine.

I've been pretty high, at times full of bliss.
The question, "I'm in the pits. How do I get out of this?"

6. Where Do They Go, Daddy?

"Daddy, who are those people sitting in the shade?
Their clothes are dirty. They make me feel afraid."
"Don't worry, Darling, we won't go too near.
Those are homeless people. There's nothing to fear.
That means they don't have anywhere to live.
Sometimes they ask if you have any money to give."
"Daddy, where do they sleep? Where do they get a drink?
If they don't take a bath, maybe they'll stink.
Where can they wash? I like my bath I've found.
Where do they go potty? There's no bathroom around."
For their bodily needs, where do they go?
In my town or a big city, I just don't know.
There are no fountains nor any public johns.
Walking into a store or gas station is frowned upon.
Most places they just can't stay around too long.
People will call the cops even when they do nothing wrong.
What a sorry state when you just don't belong.

7. Jobless

"Well, here I am at 50 years of age.
I'm pretty upset and almost in a rage.
Why, you ask, have I reached this state?
I'm unemployed. That should be enough on my plate.
As a youngster, I did what seemed right.
I graduated as an engineer, and I was bright.
In a little while I got my masters degree.
The demand was there as you'd expect it to be.

I married. We bought the house and had three kids.
Life was so good 'til the economy hit the skids.
The company downsized, and I was laid off.
The propaganda says, "Engineers are needed." I scoff.
What they mean is, "We need engineers at low pay."
Hire an old man like me, no way.
For my salary they can get two recent grads.
My experience has no value. This makes me mad.
If the young are too expensive, they can go overseas,
And get Indians or eastern Europeans if they please.
Fortunately, my wife went back to work, we're getting by.
We can pay the mortgage though we really need to try.
I've found work but at a low wage,
Competing with teenagers and immigrants at my age.
My kids are all bright. How do we send them to school?
My productive years are over. I was such a fool.
Maybe the kids should do as I should have done.
Higher education I should have shunned.
Instead be an electrician, painter, or plumber.
They seem to be the wise ones. I was dumber.
The next decade will be the most expensive of my life.
Pay for college, our mortgage, save for retirement with my wife.
What a joke life is, but I guess it's on me.
This is not how I expected this age would be.

8. Victimless Crimes 1

There's been a move to legalize certain crimes.
If no one is a victim, then is it about time?
Prostitution is a good example. Two people agree,
One pays some money, it's the sexual fee.
Let's presume the man's the one who pays.

Does he know, is the lady diseased to his dismay?
There's no way to know, is her pimp lurking nearby?
Will he be robbed at gun point? Maybe he'll die.
Does the lady know if the John is a nut?
Maybe he'll kill or maim her when the door is shut.
Besides the threat of assault, a disease can be spread.
Some are bad enough that you'll wind up dead.
A man can bring this gift home to his wife.
When she finds out, it will ruin her life.
Their marriage is destroyed. The kids also suffer.
They love both parents. Now their lives will be rougher.
Divorce also hurts grandparents and friends
Some become isolated when the marriage ends.
Even if the John is single, the diseased number will swell.
Prostitution is a victimless crime? Like hell.
The potential victims are to numerous to tell.

9. Victimless Crimes 2

A person can easily find illegal drugs if he tries.
Their suppliers are ubiquitous which is no surprise.
Legalizing would mean neither buyer nor seller is
committing a crime.
Now, possession in most cases can bring serious jail time.
What's good about the current state of affairs?
For most people the thought of prison really scares.
Otherwise, they'd be tempted to give it a try.
Just to experience the feeling of being high.
The law tries to protect the naive kid
From destroying his health like so many did.
What's wrong with the current laws as I see?
There's no control of the drug's strength or purity.

So much money can be earned with drugs,
The production and distribution is controlled by thugs.
The prisons are filled with youths who were caught.
Thousands have been killed where the drug wars are fought.
Many drugs are easy to become addicted to.
The brain and body demand that you come through.
The craving is so great all morals are set aside.
Stealing of anything from anybody, the addict will abide.
He or she will prostitute himself for the next hit.
He must satisfy the yearning and avoid the withdrawal fit.
Whatever makes it easier for drugs to use,
Would be a disaster since so many would abuse.
Maybe making penalties less severe is worth a try.
Though a true addict won't stop. He'd rather die
If the drug dealers have to find something else to do,
It won't be legitimate for these gangster crews.
With kidnapping and shake downs they'll earn their keep.
They know nothing else, being the worst of creeps.
Don't legalize drugs. Our society would really get in deep.

10. Good Turn, Feel Good?

The people at the church knew there were poor in town.
Who couldn't afford Thanksgiving dinner and felt down.
With yard sales and cake sales they raised cash.
They talked to the grocery stores. Could prices be slashed?
Arrangements were made to buy food at cost.
The stores made big contributions but not at a loss.
No one kept track of the hours spent.
Many donated money. Doing good was what it all meant.
They spread the word, that if you were in need,
Show up at the church hall for the holiday feed.

Each family would get a turkey, veggies and pie.
Not a super meal, but better than they'd normally buy.
When the big day arrived, what did they find?
Most were grateful people whom they had in mind.
Some said, "I thought it was all cooked, ready to eat.
I don't want it. It's not really a treat."
One told how they'd take it up north for a feast.
They were staying at the summer place, not chagrined in the least.
One church member watched the cars that arrived.
Later he reported about the late models they'd drive.
The saddest thing, when they cleaned the place,
Was finding food in the dumpster. What a waste!
All those people wanted to feel good about their cause,
But no good turn goes unpunished is the law.
The insult of tossing the food was the last straw.
There'd be a long wait before the next holiday meal.
No one wanted the depression they would feel.

11. In Court

Let no good turn go unpunished, it's been said.
I'm just stating a fact, without me the old guy'd be dead.
Now we're in court. His kids want to sue.
The old guy shrugged at me. What could he do?
"In you own words, could you tell us what happened that day?"
"Yes, it was lunch time, and I was on my way.
I was walking down Main, half a block west of Dundee.
I saw this old man stagger ahead of me.
I rushed up thinking it was a heart attack.
I have CPR training, so I told people to stand back.
One lady whipped out her cell to call nine-one-one.

First thing, I checked his pulse and found none.
I loosened a couple of shirt buttons and his tie,
Got in position, started, and prayed he wouldn't die.
I knew he was old, and I could break a rib.
Without CPR, he'd die. I don't mean to be glib.
In record time the rescue squad arrived.
They checked the patient, and he was alive.
A cop took ID information from me,
Thanked me for my service, then I was free.
I felt good that I'd done something worthwhile.
Then after months, I found a suit had been filed.
Now I'd like to make a statement to you.
I'd still do it the same way even knowing they'd sue,
And I hope each of you would do it too."

12. Passing By

The old guy was stretched out on the ground.
Everyone passed by. A lot of drunks were around.
All had to get to the hospital, change of shift.
Lateness was frowned upon, so their passage was swift.
A close look would have determined his state.
No vomit or wet pants, was he really an inebriate?
Then a doctor stopped, "By God, it's Chuck!"
A quick check found a pulse. He was in luck.
Dr. Charles Brown had a heart attack and fell.
No one realized that the old guy wasn't well.
After treatment and rest Chuck fully recovered.
Luckily for all, he had been discovered.
Why was it, everyone there just passed by?
Even a derelict should be helped so he doesn't die.
The Good Samaritan didn't say, "Me help? Why?"

13. No More School

Well, I graduated. I was so sick of school.
People said I wouldn't make it, but I'm no fool.
I learned to study, and to reason things out.
To know the expected answer even if in doubt.
I got that degree, in sociology no less.
I had this desire to help people I confess.
Education is damn expensive as you know.
Paying it back, what a long way to go.
I've checked everywhere looking for work,
Internet, newspaper ads, friends. I'm going berserk.
Without an income I can't find a place to stay.
Landlords want three months up front which I can't pay.
I have an old car which is about to die.
Sometimes I feel so bad I want to cry.
Well, new graduate, welcome to the adult world.
It's like a great abyss into which I've been hurled.
It seems I have two choices ahead of me,
Become a homeless bum or return to my family.
Maybe I can get a job stocking shelves in a store.
I was a waitress for a time. Could I do it some more?
If I were a guy, maybe I could mow lawns or rake.
Are those hard physical jobs more than I can take?
Just to make my day, I got a note from school.
They expect me to start repaying my loan, the new rule.
So here I am, no prospects and a mountain of debt,
But I will persevere. I'm not giving up yet.

14. Foster Kid

"Today's your 18th birthday, and I guess you know
The state stops your support. It's a low blow.

We have to set you loose. You're on your own.
Somehow in these times, there's no way you're full grown.
We can give you an old suitcase to pack.
We don't need it. You don't have to give it back.
I have a few bucks to help you get by.
Now you're an adult, so please don't cry.
You can look downtown for a job in a store.
Sometimes they hire kids to do odd chores.
Try at the YMCA. Maybe you can get a room.
They might provide it free if you push a broom.
Goodbye, Steve, and good luck in the future and all.
Just remember, pick yourself up each time you fall."
I'm afraid platitudes don't make it right.
The state is pretty cruel in my sight.
Now most kids who have a mom and dad
Are dependent 'til 26 even when the economy isn't bad.
Getting a place with three months rent up front,
Is more than most can manage in their apartment hunt.
In most areas you can't survive without a set of wheels.
Being independent is not the easiest of deals.
Those with a family have a safety net,
While for the foster kid, disaster is a good bet.
Maybe they become homeless or wind up in jail.
For the girls prostitution looms if all else fails.
Couldn't we have rooming houses as in the past,
Where a youngster could stay while his poverty lasts.

15. Adopted
"Mom, my friends keep saying something bad,
That I don't look like you or dad.

Your hair is blond, and dad's is red,
While mine is black all over my head.
My face is too round, my nose too flat.
That's what Alice says. She's such a brat.
Shouldn't I look like my parents, at least a bit?
It's sort of like, I just don't fit."
If you haven't explained about adoption to her,
Then you better be careful, that's for sure.
Certainly don't say, her first Mom didn't want her or worse,
She could have been dropped in the drowning bucket at birth.
Make up something, like her mom and dad died.
You picked her out. You were so happy you cried.
Maybe someday she'll learn the ugly facts,
But she'll know how love counted with your unselfish act.

16. Welfare Fraud

I was tired of my mom telling me what to do.
I discussed this with my friends, and they knew.
Pregnancy was the way. I got my friend Bill to do the deed.
We had sex before, so he readily agreed.
Then I talked to the school nurse about my swings in mood,
How I felt depressed sometimes or exceedingly good.
We talked to a psychologist. He was such a sap.
He decided I was bipolar, a definite handicap.
I told him how my mom was so mean to me.
He talked to the welfare people. We didn't have to plea.
They set me up in my own apartment, brand new,
At a nice location, and completely furnished too.
Welfare gave me a check and food stamps while I was there.
They explained how they'd provide free health care.
My mom said I'd never have all life's good things,

Like a car, a summer home, the pretty blings,
A fancy house, for my kids' college, a free ride.
But who knows what welfare will provide.
So far I've gotten everything that I've tried.

17. Hungarian Revolt*

The Russians had occupied his country for eleven years.
This is enough thought Jesu and his college peers.
They decided to stage a demonstration, a quiet type,
Just parade around town, but the time was ripe.
More students arrived, then workers joined in.
A demonstration in a communist country is the worst kind of sin.
The police were called to stop them but would not.
They agreed with these rebels, refusing orders on the spot.
The Russian army which occupied that land,
Was ordered to fire on the protesters out of hand.
Some did, but the majority refused to obey.
"We've won," students and workers started to say.
The Russian soldiers were pulled back. The world cheered.
But days later new troops from the east appeared.
They brought tanks which they drove along the streets.
They fired on any group they happened to meet.
Brave souls fought back. Their weapons were few.
They had dynamite workers provided and gas bombs too.
These were called Molotov cocktails, an appropriate name.
A gasoline filled bottle with a wick, and you're in the game.
The world saw an unforgettable sight,
A twelve year old boy throwing a bundle of dynamite.
Some tanks were destroyed, but infantry arrived.
Tanks and soldiers protect each other and both survive.

The world was paralyzed. There was nothing we could do.
By the time we responded, the Russians would be all
through.
Jesu heard from his friends, "The commies know who
we are.
They are rounding up and killing people. They've gone
too far."
Jesu's parents said, "You must do what's best.
Join the other rebels and flee to the west."
Hundreds of thousands fled to Austria next door.
They were resettled in many places. America took more.
The rebels gave all but their lives, brave women and men.
They'd never see family, friends, or country again.
I met Jesu in graduate school on a later day.
A Hungarian professor had helped smooth his way.
With all he had given would life ever be okay.
*Oct. 1956.

18. 15% of Workers

There are six important occupations, the four Fs, M, and C.
They produce what all people need, you and me.
Factory work, forestry, fishing, most important farming,
Mining and construction, for all, the trends are alarming.
An estimated 15% of our workers are in these fields.
They support all the rest of us with their yields.
Economists would call them the producers of wealth.
The rest are in service including those safeguarding our health,
Plus teachers and all others who are government paid,
Sales people, lawn mowers, barbers, and house maids,
Lawyers, accountants, emergency workers on call,
Bankers, nannies are samples of them all.

None of these are producers of wealth it's agreed,
Though for many of them there is truly a need.
Wealth producing jobs, for their kids, parents don't desire,
Since not being white collar, raises their ire.
The wealth producers are supporting all the rest of us,
All the service workers, the children, the retired, plus,
All those on welfare, deserving or not,
And the unemployed. This should not be their lot.
You'd think we'd support those occupations we need,
Rather than make it harder for them to succeed.
The factories are being moved to China at a fast rate,
Because of profit, the elite think this is great.
The foresters are under fire, the trees they can not cut.
Fishermen are restricted with fishing grounds shut.
Farmers have always had it hard, a life that's rough.
Construction is the first to stop when times are tough.
Miners can't mine, and drillers can't drill.
Both are subject to rabid environmentalists' will.
We don't want pipes ever or power lines in view.
About the needs for a modern life, we haven't a clue.
With all this going on, what will the future bring?
For our country, is third class status the thing?
Our economy can collapse worse than in twenty nine.
All workers including white collar will be in bread lines.
Except maybe there'll be no bread on which to dine.

19. They're Owed

My mom took care of me since the time of my birth.
There were moms before moms since the beginning of the earth.
That unbroken chain of love resulted in me.
Most everyone can say the same as it should be.

When we were young, my sister and I were good buds.
We still see each other regularly as you'd hope we would.
From the older girls who organized neighborhood games,
To the vast majority of my teachers, it's the same.
I owe so much to the females in my life,
Though none can compare to the greatest, my wife.
Our daughter was a gift, oh how she was adored.
After three boys, we thought there'd be no more.
Our sons married three great gals, the plus,
They and our daughter brought nine lovely grand
daughters* to us.
I've known many fine women coworkers and friends,
Fellow students, neighbors, the list has no end.
Now a great question clouds my mind.
Why do so many men seem to be so blind?
Females are our partners as you should expect.
We don't need to deify, but they deserve our respect.
* Plus one grandson

20. Speed Dating

A new craze among the unattached set
Is speed dating. After an evening, how many were met?
You sit across from each other for a minute or two,
You introduce yourself and mention what interests you.
When the bell rings, you move. It's part of the game.
If you are interested, you leave a phone number and name.
What can you learn with the time allowed?
Physical characteristics only, for crying out loud.
"I met this guy, sort of handsome in a rugged way.
He said he wanted marriage and kids. What a thing to say.
He's an engineer and seemed kind of shy.

Well, he's not for me. I want an exciting type guy."
She found nothing with this rapid date.
Character, age, health, what he likes, what he hates.
The most important personal traits take time to learn.
If I were there, the rules I would spurn.
Should I spot a young lady who interested me,
I'd walk up to her, introduce myself and suggest we flee.
We could go for coffee and talk awhile,
Learn a little about each other in a relaxed style.
They say good decisions can be made by an intelligent man
On insufficient evidence. He does the best he can.
He never judges on almost no evidence at all.
He needs to know more before making a call.

21. Two Styles

Moms used to say, "Go out in the fresh air and sun."
That life was good. We invented all our fun.
Moms knew the advantage of vitamin D.
Playing in the dirt seemed to help with immunity.
There was always the danger of a broken bone.
Scratches and bruises didn't mean you were accident prone.
We were asked to be back for lunch or dinner.
It was our style of life. All could be winners.
Moms worked at home and were mostly around.
They'd check outside and listen for unusual sounds.
Now parents are aware of every danger out there.
A child seems to require continuous care.
If they play outside, it's in the back of the house.
To avoid being kidnapped by some predatory louse.
Kids are walked to the bus stop, a few hundred feet.
They're met in the afternoon. No peril can they meet.

Parents try to protect kids from danger of any kind,
And yet they do a poor job as you'll soon find.
First, many rely on hired help to take their place,
Either a nanny or some day care center space.
They feed them junk food. No exercise means they get fat.
Their minds are rotted by TV, electronic games, internet,
stuff like that.
Mom drives them around while talking on the cell.
Auto accidents are kids' biggest danger you know darn well.
Older kids can have parties. They try drugs and booze.
How does this protect them from danger with all they use?
They send their young to colleges at high cost.
With no supervision kids can destroy bodies. Minds can be lost.
Now tell me which style is better for the child,
More freedom when young with dangers mild,
Or allowing them as teens to go completely wild.

22. McMansion

The neighborhood is certainly known for its trees.
Some 60 years ago our town zoned for these.
To slow rapid growth, we had large lot sizes.
As zoning measures went, this seemed rather wise.
The builder mostly put up ranches with six rooms
Which were always big enough 'til the recent building boom.
Suddenly, people want big houses. McMansions they're
called.
Builders replace the ranches. We old timers are appalled.
Each time a house comes on the market, we wonder,
Does this mean another home torn asunder?
A nearby house had a tree covered corner lot.
It was well kept. Natural gardens made a pretty spot.

As time passed the artist husband passed on.
His wife recently joined him in the great beyond.
We watched and saw what was a good sign.
The house was connected to the sewer. All was fine,
Until the clearing crew appeared on the lawn.
Now every tree on our end of the lot is gone.
That's the corner where kids waited for the bus.
They played in those woods, and moms didn't fuss.
The big rocks are gone. Even the little kids played there.
Leave no reminder. The new folks won't care.
Somehow, there ought to be a law in town.
If you have hundred foot trees, you can't cut them down.
Dear Bill and Barb, I hope you can't see
Your beautiful lot has lost every tree.
The house where you loved will no longer be.

23. What Does He Do?

Several years ago a neighbor dropped from view.
He became a hermit. I wonder, what does he do?
His wife works and his grown son as well.
I wave to them from across the street where I dwell.
They are a Chinese family and are reserved in their ways.
When we talk, asking about him wouldn't be okay.
Once a year or so, our hermit will pop out the door.
If he's been seen, he'd like to drop through the floor.
He'll zip back inside as quick as can be.
What can I make of this behavior from what I see?
I imagine he reached 50 or more years old.
His employer said goodbye. They were quite cold.
In his culture they revere men of his age.
They are treated with respect, the wise old sage.

The loss of face was more than he could bear.
So he became reclusive and has kept to his lair.
Does he read or study the learned from the past?
Maybe painting or writing in Chinese gives him a blast.
Or does he sit and stare at nothing or the TV,
Waiting day after day for the eventuality.
Another life wasted as far as I can see.

24. Fussy Eaters

Most kids are pretty fussy about what they eat.
Make sure different foods on their plates never meet.
They may like each ingredient in a casserole or stew,
But not together. They'll turn up their noses at these two.
Mostly, they prefer junk food or things raw.
Poor mom, removing fruit skin and bread crust is the law.
My mom claimed all the vitamins were in crusts and skin.
She hated the waste. Throwing these out was a sin.
She also wanted to see nothing but clean plates.
Think of those poor starving children in foreign states.
Many of those in my generation still do as she said.
Now look where waste not, want not, has lead.
Most of us frugal folks carry some extra weight.
We have to learn wasting is no sin before it's too late.
Stop eating before you're full is the new rule.
This leading to a healthier life is pretty cool.
What to do about fussy eating, I haven't a clue.
For each generation of mothers, it's up to you.

Chapter 6

Mankind has solved problems over the years.
Unfortunately, they'll keep coming, I fear.

1. The Future

I've often wondered what the future will bring.
In the past we have guessed wrong on many things.
There is the prediction that I must propose
That concerns economics. See if I hit it on the nose.
Any family knows you can spend more than you earn
Now and then, but you must reverse this you soon learn.
Our country has been exporting money for many a year.
Something will happen that sensible people fear.
Our money will lose value. Super inflation will arrive.
Foreign countries won't sell as our money's value dives.
When we no longer have oil to fuel our cars,
Most people won't work 'cause the distance is too far.
If you don't work, then you won't be paid.
Businesses will stop running unless they get government aid.
Wild inflation means any aid will do no good.
No suppliers will ship stuff even if they could.
Most critical is getting food to the masses,
But farmers need supplies, and their equipment needs gas.
After the supermarket shelves empty, it's said
Civilization lasts three days before it turns on its head.
Then the strong take from the weak 'til we all wind up dead.

2. National Debt

Currently the national debt is about 16 trillion.
That's 16 followed by 12 zeros (a million, million).
We can't really imagine numbers this grand,
So I'll put it in a form we can all understand.
If we divide it among the population of the USA,
It's about 50 grand apiece. To some this is okay.
However, let's consider the typical family of four.
Their share is some 200 grand. That's the score.
If this family has a 200 grand mortgage to pay,
They merely have to double their monthly outlay.
Being good parents they need to put money aside
For the two kids education who won't get a free ride.
Since employers don't pay toward any pension plan,
And medical insurance coverage seems banned,
This typical family can't possibly pay their "share."
It's so much worse for the truly poor out there.
Will the national debt become much worse?
Will we ever get away from this financial curse?
Unfortunately, there's no honorable way to pay the debt.
Asking the working citizens to foot the bill is a bad bet.
So we can declare bankruptcy of our nation.
We can cause the debt to lose value through wild inflation.
We can tax imports that represent our jobs lost.
Or, we can drastically cut programs of high cost.
Three of these scenarios would cause the world economy
to collapse
Since the dollar drives commerce all over the map.
There would be a loss of faith without which business
can't thrive.
This would punish damn near every person alive.

The lesson here which every being should see,
Is don't accumulate debts on thoughtless spending sprees.
Note, that if your debt gets really, really high,
You can't even pay interest no matter how you try.

3. Let's Be Like the Europeans

People have looked at Europe with an envious eye.
"They seem to have it so good," is the cry.
For want of a better name it's the welfare state.
With cradle to grave security life seems so great.
By law their governments set a high minimum wage,
Free medical care, pensions starting at an early age,
Short work weeks, vacations of a month and a half,
Free college education, and some things that seem daft.
Like the Dutch government buys paintings and other art.
One just has to call himself an artist to take part.
There's subsidized public transport and housing too.
Prosperity shouldn't be limited to the wealthy few.
Impossible to fire a worker, payments at birth and death.
It seems their governments are involved in each breath.
However, there's a result about which some have no clue.
Did the government promise too much to you?
Can your producers supply enough of the wealth
To keep your economy in a good state of health?
A country should be considered like a family.
Don't spend more than you earn on spending sprees.
For a big capitol investment it's okay to go in debt.
For normal monthly expenses it's a bad bet.
A country can go in debt when times are rough.
Fighting a war or depression are serious enough
When prosperity reigns, debt should be payed down.

Rather this than borrowing more, in debt you'll drown.
European nations collect taxes at a high rate,
For some nations it's not enough to avoid their fate.
The USA is in the same boat. Is it too late?

4. Going Green

Back in '73 the Arabs wouldn't sell us oil,
Putting the world's energy supply in real turmoil.
We were supporting Israel, and this made them boil.
Gasoline supplies were short. There were lines.
A dollar's worth per car said the signs.
Prices moved up fast, a gallon for 40 cents.
Then, people were careful how their money was spent.
There were unexpected repercussions at least for some.
These folks tried to prepare for what was to come.
Many doubled the insulation on their attic floors.
They invested in double pane windows and storm doors.
Solar hot water heaters were tried by daring types.
They had a lot to learn about materials and pipes.
The government got involved with tax breaks.
To conserve energy, you do what it takes.
Unfortunately, we learned the heaters weren't so good.
The initial cost wasn't recovered as we hoped it would.
The heater on the roof could be blown off in a storm.
For cold weather, antifreeze with heat exchanger was the norm.
It required a pump with no circulation at night.
It became more and more expensive than at first light.
Since a regular water heater was needed now and then,
The solar heater was relegated to the dust bin.
It was a lesson in wishful thinking that we should learn.

Carefully think out the whole thing unless you have
money to burn.
Free energy from the sun and wind or whatever,
Is not free. Using it requires money and you must be clever.
Maybe some day we'll get it right. I can't say never.

5. Constant Entertainment

In the not too distant past, entertainment was rare.
People provided for themselves if not busy with daily cares.
Kids organized their own activities and games.
Baseball, stickball, kick ball are some of the names,
Plus hide and seek, marbles, kick the can and tag.
If there were enough kids, then capture the flag.
There was little music unless you were among the lucky few
Who had a piano with a daughter whose fingers flew.
Your town may have had a concert band,
A theater for plays or an orator who was grand.
Maybe your entertainment was reading or playing cards,
Or conversing on the porch while surveying the yard.
Some learned the banjo. The harmonica would amuse.
It could be stored in a pocket always ready to use.
The invention of the radio caused a big change in our views.
Initially, it was for communication, like serious news.
Then for entertainment, a great discovery was made.
People could listen to programs or music remotely played.
The phonograph made it possible for you to choose
What you would listen to, classical, jazz, or blues.
This allowed you to do two things according to need.
While listening, you could drive, study, work or read.
With all the devices now available to us,
Entertainment is always there with no fuss.

However, all of it makes us distracted and alone.
Man, the social species, this should never condone.
Is this continuous stimuli good for your brain?
Interacting with your fellow men may keep you sane.
Also, the occasional need for quiet solitude is plain.

6. Immigrants

If you don't have enough concerns, I'll help you out.
Here's something you may never have thought about.
I learned about unwanted immigrants as a child.
I'll explain 'cause I don't want you going wild.
I'm talking about garden pests, the imported kind.
Japanese beetles, European corn borers were what I'd find.
Later I learned about Dutch elm disease.
Many city streets no longer have these stately trees.
One of the widest used woods in the past
Was from the chestnut tree. You'd be aghast.
It was the dominant hard wood in the northeast.
It now is rarely found, a victim of disease.
We moved to New England and found the gypsy moth,
Purposefully imported to make silk cloth.
Now as I age, they're increasing the pace.
Med flies, killer bees, fire ants in various places.
Ravenous termites destroying houses down New Orleans way.
These darn unwanted guests make us pay.
Varmints are after hemlocks, maples, oak, and spruce.
Should we just give up and say what's the use?
Ash trees have their bug, so does the western pine.
Even the hearty aspen may be hard to find.
All these have insects imported from across the sea.
Will we reach the point where we lose every tree.

Bigger beasties to our shore are also new.
Burmese pythons, walking catfish, and lampreys to name a few.
The latest was imported by well meaning guys.
Chinese carp clean rivers, but there's a surprise.
They're displacing native fish and are out of control.
This result was certainly not the goal.
Some plants are also of the invasive type.
Norway maple, loose strife, and the burning bush get the hype.
With all the varmints, I won't worry about these.
Maybe if worse comes to worse, they'll replace the dead trees.

7. Cheap Medicine

I read a well known doctor's claim years ago.
The best medicine is when you keep costs low.
He compared treating polio with an iron lung,
Against the cost of vaccine before the disease had begun.
Few people could be treated the expensive way,
So if your lungs were affected, most could only pray.
Now much of the research is the expensive type.
Using stem cells to grow new organs gets the hype.
There's talk of genetic "corrections" for some disease.
Individual treatment for each patient are among these.
With medical costs currently taking 16% of the GDP,
Can you imagine what future costs will be?
Will they try to replace every worn out heart,
So every old person can have a new start.
Replace every liver, lung, kidney, and joint.
There's no way they can do this is my point.
So will the super treatments be only for the rich,
While the rest will be left to moan and bitch?
I can't help feeling, medicine should be to treat the young.

Growing a new heart should save a life just begun.
For the old, emphasize prevention like vaccines.
Exercise, eat properly, lead a life that's clean.
Work hard, play hard, find love, avoid stress.
Maybe with luck you can live a life that's blessed,
And stay pretty healthy 'til the day you die.
This is the inexpensive way we all should try.

8. How Far?

Life is a journey in time but also in space.
We may live in one spot but travel all over the place.
I'm pushing 80 so you can gage what I say.
I've estimated the distance in each different way.
I've walked all my life especially as a youth.
An average of one mile a day is the truth.
This is more than enough to circle the earth.
Bicycle, boat, and train trips aren't enough to have worth.
Bus travel has mounted with trips as I age.
I have circled the earth again at this late stage.
I've flown a lot both for work and for fun.
This counts as four circles that I've done.
Like all of us, I just love travel by car.
My 24 auto circles wins this contest by far.
My total is 30 trips circumnavigating our orb.
This boggles my mind, too much to absorb.
About the journey and to complete this rhyme,
So far my heart has beaten three billion times.

9. Survival in the Wild*

I've heard this remark from more than one.
"Look around you and see all we have done.

The environment is screwed up. The earth won't last.
We should live like the Native Americans did in the past."
We could make this a challenge for them to try.
Is it possible to survive? Could they get by?
I'll make a partial list of what you'd do without.
I can start with food. This alone should make you doubt.
No orange juice, no milk, no cocoa, coffee or tea,
No eggs, bacon, sausage, or toast will you see.
No bananas, Danish or muffins, no jelly or jam,
Forget the cereal, pancakes, waffles and ham.
That's just breakfast. Shall we go on to lunch.
Not one salad vegetable, no sandwich to munch.
We take for granted damn near everything we eat.
I'll tell you what you could expect. None are a treat.
Various roots are edible like skunk cabbage and cat tails.
Others you may find. Inventiveness must prevail.
For fruit there are various berries, none in abundance.
There's blue, black, straw and others you may find by chance.
Wild grapes are good, but spit out the skin and seeds.
These fruits are available for a short time of your need.
Nuts of various types and seeds can be found
Carefully prepare those acorns which in places abound.
You can get meat and fish, but you must follow the rules.
You have to make gear and traps without metal tools.
Grubs and insects are nourishing you'll find.
You'll have to get used to raw stuff. You'll never dine.
But why worry about food, the priority that's first
Is finding clothing since freezing is the worst.
Only deer, moose and bear have enough fur

To keep you alive over the winter for sure.
For shelter construct a hut, at least you can try.
Tree bark is about it, to keep you dry.
There's one basic fact to keep in mind,
Nothing manufactured allowed, only stuff you find.
Actually, it doesn't matter what you do.
Lyme disease will get everyone including you.
If our civilization should collapse, no one will survive.
There's just not enough to keep us alive.
*In the northeast forest including lakes, swamps, etc.

10. Raising Sea Levels

Global warming is with us. How bad will it get?
No one really knows, utter chaos or a little sweat.
We do know what will happen if the world's glaciers melt.
The resulting disaster will be widely felt.
The rising sea will inundate coastal areas and more.
Inland inhabitants wonder, "Will my property be on the shore?"
It's possible to calculate how much the sea level will rise,
For one percent of glacier melt*, four feet is the size.
This would cause big problems especially with a storm surge.
Even with dikes, land would be submerged.
The effort of protecting New York with dikes
Means damming the Hudson, East River and the likes.
Multiply the damage caused by a hurricane of category one
By a big factor. There's tremendous damage done.
On the coast there's a dozen major cities in the USA.
Plus smaller cities and towns along the way.
We can't protect them from a sea level rise of four feet.

Of all possible scenarios this is the least.
If all the world's glaciers should melt,
A devastating four hundred foot rise would result.
Every coastal country of the entire earth
Would have it's economy shattered for all it's worth.
*Or calving. Melting sea ice doesn't count.
Think of Archimedes Principle.

11. Climate Change

Over the millennia there have been many climate changes.
These are cyclical with wide temperature ranges.
The cold part of the cycles are called ice ages.
Mile thick glaciers cover the north during this stage.
The sea level drops with all the ice on land.
During the warm period glaciers melt and the seas expand.
The last ice age ended some 12 thousand years ago.
We've been in a warming trend, but change has been slow.
That is until man progressed to the modern date,
When we started burning coal and oil at a fast rate.
We are changing the atmosphere with CO_2 and methane gas,
Which both "trap" heat like greenhouse glass.
Warming radiation from the sun can get to earth,
But of cooling radiation outward there is a dearth.
We are all aware of the rising level of the sea.
Storms will get worse. The Arctic will become ice free.
Many species will be affected and may become extinct.
Man will suffer, and his numbers will shrink.
One effect not mentioned about climate change,
Desert regions of the earth will extend their range.
Man is inventive. All we can hope is brains win out.
Else wise, there'll be utter disaster with no doubt.

12. Knowledge Lost

A great cataclysm occurred and most of mankind died.
The few remaining wanted to live. They really tried.
Though they had none of the skills of ancient men,
Enough material was available from what had been.
Food, clothing, lodging and tools lasted for awhile.
The residue of the past finally gave out, then the trial.
They found by experiment many edible plants.
Hunting skills were developed often by chance.
They invented what they required to stay alive.
No need to emphasize, it was hard to survive.
The old passed down stories of the glories of the past.
To explain stone structures and other relics they passed.
The young wondered, all was beyond their ken.
Their imagination couldn't fathom way back when.
None of them would ever know what was lost.
Knowledge gained over millennia was the cataclysm's cost.
The knowhow of a million occupations gone.
Science and technology developed since civilizations
dawn.
Would mankind rise to the good life again?
Maybe with time he'd return where he'd been.
Though one thing would be different the second time around.
All the easily gotten resources can no longer be found.
This one fact might just keep mankind down.

13. Replacements

What if something happened to eliminate the human race.
Would another species evolve to take our place?
Some make claims like they truly know.
We had a common ancestor with chimps 5 million years ago.

They and their cousins, bonobos, stand the best chance
Of becoming intelligent like humans at first glance.
That's if the right changes occur at the right times.
None of us know what was important in our own ancient climes.
Did ice ages and hot spells stimulate our changes?
Did movement of game or hard times extend our ranges?
Whatever happens, it would take eons it's clear.
Though pathogens, predators or famine may interfere.
It's been suggested that raccoons may be next in line.
They're smart and dexterous. Both are good signs.
Who knows what will happen with the passage of time.

14. Needs of Intelligent Life

I'm impressed by what we can train animals to do.
Of chimps and dolphins this is certainly true.
Maybe with evolution over millions of years
Chimps could be considered humankind's peers.
However, dolphins will never make the grade.
Their water environment limits any progress that could be made.
I have thought about what a species would need
On some planet anywhere, to evolve and succeed.
First liquid water is necessary for living things.
Soluble nutrients (water has most) is what it brings.
This means the temperature if truth be told,
Like for Goldilocks, it must not be too hot nor too cold.
So the planet has to be the right distance from its star.
Too hot if it's too close, too cold if too far.
This planet should have the right ratio of sea to land,
Sea to spawn life and land on which life can expand.

The planet should not be too big and not too small.
Too much gravity, and you die if you fall,
Too little and your atmosphere is lost in space.
Liquid water would follow at a fast pace.
Various elements should be present in the right amounts.
Oxygen, carbon and hydrogen are those that really count.
All life on earth requires these three.
Others like calcium are important to a lesser degree.
For a species to progress beyond a primitive state,
Metal ores should be plentiful and easy to locate.
Iron makes generation of electricity possible for one,
Plus structures, tools, and machines when civilization's begun.
Plants and animals have provided for man's needs.
Anywhere in the universe this is necessary to succeed.
With all these qualifications will intelligent life be there,
If we explore our galaxy nearby or everywhere?
Then if we consider intelligent life's development state,
On each planet life may evolve at a different rate.
Considering man's brief time here at home,
Does anyone think we'll find anyone however far we roam?

15. Will We Fly to the Stars?

Maybe in the future, we'll try to send men to Mars.
If this is successful. Then next it's the stars.
Planning to get the volunteers there and back
Will require capabilities that we now lack.
For instance living with no gravity causes bones to decay.
They lose strength. It get worse by the day.
There are only a few solutions the engineers could use.
Fly under power or have a ship truly huge,
Which would rotate to get centrifugal force.

Both solutions need excessive fuel of course.
The gravitation force is replaced in both cases.
Maybe we could medicate the men while in space.
Hibernation's not natural though they might try that.
The only true hibernating mammals are bats.
In space we must take what we need besides gear,
Food, water, and air to last at least a year.
The two way trip needs a ship of some complication,
Most likely assembled at an orbiting space station.
The space craft would start out with five parts,
A booster which impels it, drops away near the start.
The remainder would travel for months on end.
After decelerating it will orbit our planet friend.
Two parts will drop to reach the ground.
One of these will be where the Mars base is found.
The other will take the astronauts back up in space
To the orbiting station, their return base.
Finally, the last module will return them to earth,
Where they'll rendezvous with the initial satellite and berth.
This brief description would only be for Mars flights.
No other planet is suitable in my sight.
What are the chances of flying to another star?
With today's technology*, they're just too far.
Our nearest neighbor, four light years away
Would take fifty thousand years. On earth we'll stay.
* Or foreseeable improvements.

16. 10,000 Years from Now

Predicting that far in advance may be too hard to do.
Remembering 10,000 years in the past could give us a clue.
All those years ago humans had invented the important stuff,

Clothing, shelter, containers, tools to make life less tough.
They had domesticated dogs and started agriculture I'd bet.
Their villages probably weren't permanent just yet.
Now change seems to have accelerated so much,
We have personal computers, cell phones and such.
Few of the modern things were guessed 50 years ago,
And no one can guess technologically ahead I know.
So I'll summarize what the next 10,000 years will bring.
I expect overpopulation will be the first big thing.
Massive famine will wipe out a large part of the human race.
All it will take is crop failures in a few places.
This can be caused by insects, pathogens, or drought.
There's not enough "extra" food to keep this demon out.
We will run out of most of our natural resources.
At least there will be no easy sources.
Certain metals are just too hard to replace.
What happens when petroleum is reduced to a trace.
Pathogens will always cause misery and death.
They mutate so easily, new ones arrive with each breath.
Of course, there's economic collapse when nothing works.
This may be the first big change and society goes berserk.
People worry about global warming, would it be so bad,
Considering everything else that I just said?
Coastal cities would be wiped out by rising sea.
Maybe a billion or more people would have to flee.
There's talk of space travel, maybe settling Mars.
Everywhere else is just too inhospitable or too damn far.
Forget discovering inhabited planets far in space.
We'll never be able to communicate with such a race.
My hope is that humanity can prepare,

And use collective intelligence to solve problems out there.
I don't expect beneficial mutations to appear,
Since it's claimed humans haven't changed in 50,000 years.
So there will be no super smart future men.
We'll have to get by with what we have even then.
Maybe human beings will live like our stone age kin.

Chapter 7

So much caused by fate, others, or our own hand,
And yet mankind survives. We can withstand.

1. Life's Woes

When I write and reread all these tales of woe,
I feel how blessed I am, more than anyone would know.
There's heartache for me when tragedy hits.
Even when I'm not directly affected, it's the pits.
All should feel bad when someone's spouse dies.
When a child suffers, everyone cries.
We all know that sickness and pain will strike,
Relatives, neighbors, friends and the like.
This is part of life. To avoid it, the only way
Is to isolate yourself completely every day.
To me, the ache of a lonely life,
With no family, especially no wife,
Would be infinitely worse than the loss
Of a loved one. I'd rather bear pain's cross.
Sickness and death are there for all.
We have to bear it when the fates call.
Personally, my life has been filled with joy.
I will cling to this attitude like a buoy.
Maybe I'm an idiot, just a simple man,
But looking for the good will remain my plan.

2. A Child's Message

The Christmas Pageant was to be performed in a week.
Little Billy was shy, and could he speak?
Such a nice, sweet boy. He should have a part.
Could he learn his lines? He certainly has the heart.
The teacher mulled this over in her mind,
Then had a great idea, a part she did find.
"He can be the inn keeper. There's just one line.
I'll get him started. Now we won't be in a bind."
Billy was happy and practiced again and again.
"There's no room at the inn," he said it then
He repeated it some more 'til it sounded just right.
He was fully prepared for that wondrous night.
The auditorium was full of parents and friends,
Grandparents and siblings, people without end.
Then it began. There was anticipation all around.
All looked at the stage, and none made a sound.
Mary and Joseph approached the inn door.
They asked the inn keeper, "Is there one room more?"
"There's no room at the inn," Billy said with a loud clear voice.
The couple turned away. Was there another choice?
Then a plaintive call that came out as a boom,
"You can come to my house. You can stay in my room."
Well, that one simple line brought the audience to their feet,
This shy young boy had said something so sweet,
It will always be remembered, a Christmas time treat.
It has been said, "A child shall show them the way,"
And so it was on that memorable day.

3. Love Story

"The poor thing. Someone shot him. He can't fly."
"Honey, he's a wild goose. He just might die."
"Can't we help him. I can bandage the wing.

I'll feed and water him. I could make a sling."
The girl took care of her pet goose all winter long.
He got better. He accepted his life and got pretty strong.
But he would never fly again. It's what geese do.
When spring came, the changing season made him blue.
A flock passed over returning to the north.
The plaintive honking brought a lone flyer forth.
A female landed. It was love at first sight.
She stayed. There were babies. It seemed so right.
"You know Honey, things may change. Fall will come.
They're used to migrating. He'll be so glum."
The female and the grown young flew south one day.
Mom had to show the young ones the way.
The pet goose did seem sad for a while.
Time passed with the winter. Then spring brought out a smile.
One day the female returned and dropped from the sky.
They continued their romance as the warm season passed by.
Every year they repeated their annual rites.
Though just birds, a true love story in our sight.

4. Burn Victim

The crash was horrific, the fire intense.
Fortunately, a passerby was brave and used his sense.
He donned his gloves and wrapped his scarf around his face,
As he ran to the crash with the utmost haste.
He opened the door and reached to unlatch the belt.
The women was conscious, but what pain she felt.
Her winter clothes had protected her from the fire
Except for her face. There the effects were dire.
The rescuer carried her back up to the road.
Another good Samaritan had called the 911 code.

People put their coats down to soften her bed,
To keep her warm, and to cushion her head.
The emergency crews arrived, medical, fire and cops.
The victim was driven away. They took out the stops.
She would live, this was without a doubt.
The pain would diminish, but would she make out?
Our victim was recently married. To add to the pain,
Her young husband left her. Could he ever explain?
He had found her attractive. He married for her looks.
Now he couldn't face what the fire took.
Her insurance provided for her immediate need.
In growing new skin, by and large they did succeed.
She needed extensive work to rebuild her face.
With no insurance or money this would not take place.
Then a young plastic surgeon heard of her
And made a commitment about which he was sure.
He had the time, and he had the skill.
He would work free of charge. There'd be no bill.
Her wedding picture was used as his guide.
Many operations were needed to restore the bride.
He took tissue from here and cartilage from there.
Even vaginal skin provided new lips with care.
With his tenderness and devotion, she was drawn to him.
He admired her strength, her vigor and vim.
After all the operations, the last bandage was removed.
The young doctor's skill at rebuilding was proved.
He stood back, admired his work, then made his request.
"I love you so much, please marry me. I would be blest."
"Oh, yes, yes, yes," she answered with a bit of laughter.
As in the fairy tales, they lived happily ever after.

5. Love Amongst Destruction

On the east end of Normandy, the Brits landed.
They met little resistance, so their beachhead expanded.
Then the Germans fought back as reinforcements arrived.
Casualties mounted. The wounded who survived
Were carried to the beach to wait evacuation.
It seemed endless to Ian. It was a bad situation.
The pain was getting bad. The medics had too much to do.
Then an angel appeared. A young lady came into view.
Marie was just 16. She announced to her Mere.
I'm going to help those poor men down there.
She wasn't a nurse, she wasn't trained,
But she could comfort the fallen and reduce their pain.
Ian saw Marie, and his pain eased.
For some magical reason his heart was seized.
Language was a problem, but he made his meaning clear.
He promised before God and all he held dear,
After Germany's defeat and the end of this strife,
He would return to France and make her his wife.
Ian had recovery to do. For him the war was over.
He spent his recuperation time beyond the Cliffs of Dover.
Ian was discharged from the army after the war ended.
He still limped but by and large he was mended.
He made his way back to the village in France.
The lovely Marie knew Ian at first glance.
She knew that he had meant what he said.
He would be back, and then they'd be wed.
This is one fairy tale that really came true.
From the horror of war love came to these two.

6. Internment

The war had started. Everything looked bad.
They had attacked our fleet. We were damn mad.
Pearl Harbor was littered with ships damaged and sunk.
Without warning they attacked, then away they slunk.
All around the Pacific there were disasters.
The Japs were showing everyone who were the masters.
Where was their Grand Fleet? Would they hit the west coast?
People were afraid, Californians more than most.
Japanese immigrants among them, seemed like a threat.
Were they spies? It would be a good bet.
We rounded up the Japs by presidential order.
They packed suitcases and moved with no disorder.
They went to the camps leaving most everything behind.
These were like military bases. For home they pined.
Their needs were provided for, but they couldn't leave.
It was better than in other countries you should believe.
Though understandable, this was among the worst we did
at the time,
Not only imprisoned without a trial, but without a crime.
There they stayed for most of the war,
Even though their young volunteered, patriots to the core.
When they were released, it was like a new dawn.
Then they found possessions and businesses were gone.
These Japanese were gardeners and tillers of land.
Common folk though their work was considered grand.
They reassessed their lives and tried something new.
They sent their kids to college like the well off do.
In a few years they prospered. They were on the ball.
Of ethnic groups they became most educated of all.
Their incomes matched this. They became well to do.
Occasionally, the bad old leads to the good new.

7. Tipping

There's a car stopped. I wonder, is she all right?
It's a flat tire and getting on toward night.
I better stop. Not many coming along this way.
She's older. Hope I don't scare her this time of day.
I'll stand back a bit, so I won't be threatening with my attire.
"Ma'am, I'd like to help you. I'll change your tire.
Just pop the trunk. I'll get what I need."
And so he completed the job with ease and speed.
"You should be okay. I'm glad we met."
"Young man, can I give you something. I'm in your debt."
"No, no, I can't. Just pass it on if you can."
As he drove off, she thought, what a nice young man.
She stopped at a roadside diner for a bite to eat.
Her server was a lovely young lady who looked dead on
her feet.
The young lady was very pregnant and needed a lift.
After finishing her meal, she decided to leave a gift.
"A nice young man said to pass it on," said a note.
A hundred dollar bill punctuated what she wrote.
Later that evening, the young couple talked about the day,
The lady with her tire who he helped send on her way.
Then it dawned on them. She had done as he said,
And passed on the good deed. This is where it lead.
Now paying this month's rent would cause less dread.

8. Don't Ever Give Up

In the early fifties Eric was just a kid of four.
Polio was a scourge. Soon there'd be no more.
For young Eric the vaccine came too late.
He survived, but crippling was his fate.

His poor little legs were wasted away.
Mom and Dad decided a cripple he would not stay.
Regular massage helped though he was carried everywhere.
Eric couldn't even stand. His weight he couldn't bear.
Several operations helped to make those legs strong.
At age six braces were fitted. It was still hard to get along.
As Eric grew he gained upper body strength.
With crutches his strides grew in length.
It was not uncommon in that age and day
To see a muscular young man with half crutches making his way.
In college a coach noticed Eric was a gymnastics sort.
He became a champion when he took up that sport.
Maybe Eric's can do attitude was an acquired trait.
His folks certainly helped to determine his fate.
Eric studied science and finished med school
He was smart and educated and had the tools.
When he met a young boy with autism, he
Decided that's what his life's work would be.
Maybe of another crippling condition, we'll become free.

9. A Real Friend

"Mom, Mom, I have to help a friend.
She has a real problem. For herself she cannot fend.
If she tells her folks, they'll just throw her out.
It's because she's pregnant, and there is no doubt.
The clinic's open tomorrow. I can drive her there.
She doesn't have enough money. I can provide a share."
"Honey, you are a true friend. Let me talk to Dad.
He'll give you what's needed. To help he'll be glad."
And so a whole family helped this unknown friend.

Maybe they saved her from an unfortunate end.
You may not agree with what was done here.
It was the lesser sin. Choices are not always so clear.

10. The Chickadee

The two preteen boys wanted to learn wood craft skills.
Not only how to survive, but to prosper if you will,
How to find food and shelter when lost and alone,
The knowledge that allows you to get by on your own.
One boy's grandfather was Native American by birth.
He would teach them all he knew and its worth.
Mostly, they should observe and remember what they see.
What the animals do, from the deer to the lowly bee.
They should pick a special animal to be their spirit friend,
One that would teach them how to fend.
After observing and with study, they picked the chickadee.
This may seem strange to those who don't clearly see.
These little birds are tough since they stay the winter through.
Flying low out of the wind is one thing they do.
They find their food each season of the year.
No matter what, they project the appearance of cheer.
The wise old Indian was impressed with their choice.
It showed more wisdom than you'd expect from two boys.
I agree with this based on what I have seen.
I must relate two stories so you'll know what I mean.
I was building an addition and working inside.
A chickadee hit the glass. I thought he had died.
He'd flown in an open window and was flying out.
The glass was invisible to him no doubt.
In no way could he have survived a crash like that.
I picked up the little guy. In my hands he sat.

Then he stirred. He had been knocked cold.
Soon he flew to a ladder, on a rung he took hold.
Of the giant, he seemed to have no fear.
I weighed maybe 10,000 times the little dear.
Then it was out the open window, apparently okay.
Talk of toughness, that's what I would say.
The second story concerns a trait I never knew.
Birds don't provide for the future. It's generally true.
But the wise chickadee stores sunflower seeds,
Tucked under roof shingles for their future needs.
This was discovered when I reshingled my roof.
Who else did it? I needed no other proof.

11. The Voice

James' dad took off before he was born.
Mom didn't feel she needed time to mourn.
She took James north seeking her parents' aid.
Compared to alternatives, he had it made.
As James grew, a speech impediment arose.
He stuttered, the brain-mouth connection froze.
Most think stuttering is cured as you grow.
But many are cursed forever. It doesn't go.
"G-G-Gram, the other k-k-kids tease me.
W-w-what can I d-d-do, so they'll let me be?"
His teacher scolded the kids. They felt sorry.
She planned a procedure to alter the story.
James should write poetry, then memorize it.
He would recite it in class. He improved7 a bit.
He started to take lessons in drama.
Memorizing lines greatly reduced the stammer.
James finished college and was an officer in the service.

Then pursued a lifetime of acting, no thought of being nervous.
He's always prepared and thinks carefully before he speaks.
James remembers his youth when life was bleak,
"One of the hardest things for me along life's way,
Was having words in my heart that I couldn't say."
He's known for his voice, especially in Star Wars and Lion King,
That commanding delivery, the deep tone is his thing.
Who's this man who I say stands alone?
Why it's none other than James Earl Jones.
The way to overcome adversity, he has shown.

12. Essence

The basic person is our essence we could say,
But not on the molecular level like our DNA.
I suppose this includes our physique and size,
Voice, facial characteristics, coloring of hair and eyes.
In an ideal world, none of this should ever count,
Unless our own bad feelings of ourselves mount.
Our essence certainly can be affected by others,
Hurt caused by "friends", a spouse, fathers and mothers.
About our "imperfections", we may feel bad,
Too tall, too short, or too stocky, make us sad.
Maybe we're not as handsome or pretty as we want.
Are we jealous of those who are really too gaunt?
As we grow up, by a personality type we're enveloped.
Extrovert or introvert, maybe pessimist we develop.
No matter, we can always be honest and kind.
We can smile and be helpful if we are of mind.
Maybe there are chance things in life we can't control,
And changing someone else can never be our goal.

We can change our own essence. It's never too late.
Like the poem "Invictus" says, we are masters of our fate.

13. What a Way to Go

Dad was old. The calendar didn't lie.
Mom already passed. Only a few weeks had gone by.
For over 80 years they had been best friends.
That childhood romance lasted to the end.
Dad had Alzheimer's and sickness that comes with age.
He faced his fate with unbridled rage.
I helped him with meals. Stuff he liked a lot.
This lessened his rage. The treats hit the spot.
No worries now about calories, sugars, or fat.
He said I was a good son, the first I'd heard that.
Soon he didn't remember me. He no longer ate.
His kidneys failed which sealed his fate.
The doctor said they could add a month, but why.
Renal failure was a good way to die.
My siblings agreed to stop treatment for Dad.
The end was coming and none were sad.
His breath became shallower, intermittent for a while
And ended with a sigh and the trace of a smile.
My crotchety old Dad was so peaceful now.
When you're old and it's time, this is how.
No fighting to extend that last breath.
Just dignified serenity with a natural death.

14. The Greatest

I am the greatest emperor the world has ever seen.
I found the theory of everything. Scientists know what I mean.
The cure of cancer of every type is my claim.

I am the world's greatest athlete in the Olympic Games.
I am the head of the church, the revered Pope.
I developed cheap renewable energy, mankind's hope.
Here is a humble man. What have you done?
"My wife just gave birth. A new life was begun.
I swear before God, I'll raise him the best I can."
"Hear this world. Of all these, he's the best man.
All pales in comparison to this event.
The miracle of a new life is heavenly sent."

15. Dog's Life

I live with my two alphas. We three make a pack.
I came here from a far away land way back.
That other life was different. I can hardly recall.
I had a litter of pups. They were so small.
One day they disappeared. I was sad for a bit.
Then I went to this strange place. It was the pits.
Dogs and cats were kept in these cages.
They cut my belly, and it hurt for ages.
Then I was put on a truck, hell on wheels.
We were scared. You can't imagine how it feels.
Everyone barked, and some of us cried.
It was so noisy, I couldn't sleep though I tried.
After the longest time, my pack met the truck.
They were nice to me. I couldn't believe my luck.
We drove for a while and came to their den.
This was the nicest place I've ever been.
The bigger alpha, the boss, takes care of me.
We go for walks, but he doesn't let me free.
I get good food to eat, and there are treats.
I can sleep where I want. This can't be beat.

I love my pack and protect them I must.
I guard them. In me they can truly trust.
That's why in the front of the house I rest.
That's my post, and always I do my best.
I bark at anything that comes too near.
They all run away when my bark they hear.

16. The Miracle of Birth

Miracles are what I'd call unexplained good events.
They may be chance or may be heaven sent.
Past miracles might be explained through scientific thought.
Though I have a feeling this would come to naught.
There is one miracle we can partly explain,
Though it's so complicated it strains my brain.
This is the miracle of birth. How does it work?
It's the same for all mammals for what it's worth.
For humans this happens some 100 million times a year.
Hopefully, all these parents welcome it with cheer.
For the ignorant it's a straight forward and simple bet.
The more we find out, the more complicated it gets.
First, every female is born with the full compliment of eggs.
They wait 'til her body is ready near early teenage.
Then about once a month eggs ripen, mostly just one.
Multiple eggs could mean multiple births are begun.
Each egg has a full 46 chromosomes to start,
But 23 of them migrate to the egg wall and depart.
The fertilizing sperm provides the missing 23.
This resulting egg is the future baby to be.
The egg travels and embeds on the uterine wall,
Though it has no means of locomotion at all.
Now begins the true miracle of birth.

That single egg divides for all it's worth.
From one type cell more than 100 types arise.
Somehow all the body parts grow, no surprise.
All these parts are where they're supposed to be.
No one can explain this as far as I can see.
Another wonder is the characteristics the baby displays.
Different from brothers and sisters in many ways.
Mom's bone structure, Dad's eyes, Uncle Joe's chin,
Grandma's hair, Grandpa's ears, Aunt Rose's skin.
Each individual shares family traits we find,
But each is unique among all mankind.
The greatest of the unique properties is the human mind.

17. Mental Skills

What a wondrous thing is the human mind.
It has unbelievable capabilities you will find.
I've always been highly impressed with the piano protegee.
The eyes see, the brain directs, and the fingers play.
All this occurs without conscious thought,
And even fairly young with time can be taught.
Being a guy with ten thumbs, typing is also a wondrous thing.
I watch all fingers make the keyboard sing.
Now here's the conundrum, how can this be
Since such skills weren't needed through history.
Certainly evolution played absolutely no part.
Such dexterity wasn't needed for survival from the start.
Yet the brain has adapted to the modern world.
Will this continue as the future is unfurled?

18. Test of Meanness

In an embarrassing situation, what should you do?
If you honestly answer, it tells a lot about you.
I worked in an office building back in the day,
And witnessed something, an example of what I say.
I was about to walk out my office door,
When a passing secretary's slip fell to the floor.
What would you do in the situation I found?
Maybe holler, "Ha, ha, look at Judy's slip on the ground."
Or ask if you can help and hope she won't cry.
Or make believe you saw nothing and quickly walk by.
Or step back so she thinks no one saw,
And never ever mention her faux pas.
Instinctively, I chose the last option. I was right.
Why cause unnecessary embarrassment from that sight?
Unfortunately, too many would point and laugh,
With no thought of the hurt from that silly gaff.
Kids seem programmed to react in this way.
There's no empathy. They don't realize it's not play.
The secretary apparently stepped out of her slip,
Retrieved it with agility and didn't trip.

19. The Lesson

Along about seventy years ago, we were told
About one of our classmates, in no way a scold.
Bill, an epileptic, wasn't in school that day.
That's why our teacher said what she had to say.
We were told about seizures and why he was not well.
We should help him not to hit his head if he fell.
To my knowledge no one ever gave a hard time to Bill,
And we never saw a seizure to test our skill.

I wonder if teachers ever tell the kids today
That they should help those who are different in some way.
When I hear about the in-crowd and those outs,
Plus the bullies, I have my doubts.

20. The Apology

"I hope Ralph is home. I know this is the house.
After all these years, I want to apologize for being a louse.
I hear someone coming. I'll give it a go.
Hey, Ralph, remember me, Bill Bigalow."
"Yeah, I remember. Just what do you want?
Did you come to continue the old tease and taunt?"
"Ralph, I came to apologize for what I did.
I was so nasty and mean as a kid.
You've read about people with a bucket list.
I decided to do things that over the years I missed.
I have felt sorry about how we were in school.
We tried to be so cool, but it turned out pretty cruel.
I'm apologizing when appropriate and saying thanks to some
Who gave me a chance after I acted so dumb.
Ralph, if you don't accept my apology, it's okay.
I just hope life has been good to you along the way
And if you've hit hard times, I'll help you if I may.
That's about it. It's all I have to say."

21. The Tycoon's Secret

Everyone thought they knew him. They thought he was gruff.
With all his business dealings he was also tough.
James, his chauffeur, knew this wasn't completely true.
They were friends and trusted each other through and through.

One day the tycoon asked James to do a good deed.
"I want to help that young boy who's in need.
Operations can fix his deformed foot and make him well.
I'll pay whatever the cost, but please don't tell.
I want no one to know about this aid.
So promise you'll never reveal the gift I've made."
James took care of the arrangements and so it was done.
The boy and his family wondered who was the one,
But James never wavered. He relayed the thanks.
The anonymous donor's identity was always a blank.
So the tycoon maintained his gruff reputation
While quietly continuing his charitable donations.
Then there's the rest of the story to tell.
The anonymous style kept his privacy quite well.
Continuous entreaties and petitions, were easier to quell.

22. The EMT

"Where am I? What happened?" the old man boomed.
"The rescue squad brought you to the emergency room.
It seems you had a heart attack. You were lying on the ground.
A passer by called in from where you were found."
"Where's my dog? She's the best friend I ever had.
We look out for each other. I'm feeling pretty sad.
We never missed our walks three times a day,
And as a result I've been healthy you could say.
You've got to help. Is there someone we can call?"
"You're getting stressed. It's only a dog after all."
Not the right response. An EMT heard, what luck.
"Sir we have your dog. She's outside in our truck.
She's okay. I'm going to take care of her for you.
My kids will love to have her. That's what we'll do,

When you're better, you'll get her right away.
I'll come back to see you every day."
For this guy it's more than a job you see,
He takes it seriously, be the best you can be.

23. The Veterinarian

I've always liked animals. It's why I became a vet.
If you love them, they'll return love. It's a sure bet.
I've gotten my share of scratches and bites.
This is understandable. Fear means flee or fight.
Of reptiles, fish and their ilk, I've never been fond.
Unlike mammals and birds, they don't respond.
It's a tough job. They can't tell you where there's pain.
It's a lot of guess work and using the old brain.
I love to see a pet recover due to my work.
They get back the old vigor and perk.
However, there's one part of the job I really hate,
When an old pet comes in, and it's just too late.
Anything I can do will extend life for a short time.
Keeping them going, helpless and in pain, is a crime.
I usually suggest euthanizing them and yet,
This is not the reason I became a vet.
It's not professional of me, but I also shed tears.
I truly share a family's pain as death nears.
That's why I developed an adoption agency over the years.
You can't replace a loved one, but new love can start.
There's always room in your house and in your heart.

24. Pet Needs

The old guy was sitting by the side of the road.
His pet sat beside him. His age also showed.
I saw a sign as I drove by which read,
"Will work for dog food." That's what it pled.
I know there are shelters where the homeless can go.
They don't allow pets, and that's a flat out no.
Maybe these two old timers had been buddies for years,
Or they just adopted each other, two homeless peers.
I stopped to see if I could provide some aid.
When I see an animal in need, my reticence fades.
"Sir, I'll buy some food for your dog if I could.
Hey, Fella, are you okay? You don't look so good.
Has he seen a vet to check him out?"
"Not for a while, a couple of years or there about."
"Let me call my friend. He's a vet and a good man.
He'll examine the dog. I'll pay. That's my plan."
I made my call. Then we three got on our way.
The vet did his thing, but needed to keep him for a day.
"I'll take you to the shelter. Pick you up at noon.
You can get a good meal, a bath, it'll be a boon."
I made some stops for things the dog lacked.
Dog food, a water bowl, and a special backpack.
As expected, the pet had a case of intestinal worms,
Which was easier to treat than getting rid of germs.
I saw the two friends off, two for the road.
Both felt much better, in their steps it showed.
An occasional good turn can lighten a load.

25. Life's Journey

The concept of life being a journey never occurred to me
Until I was well into adulthood as it should be.
When a child, such thoughts were well beyond my ken.
Things were as they were, as they had always been.
I was not aware that anything in life changed.
All seemed static, and this didn't seem strange.
Mom, Dad, my sister and I were all
Except there was our dog when I was small.
I didn't know of new life 'til the dog gave birth.
I could watch pups grow in length and girth.
It dawned on me that in time we grow,
That the next year would be different somehow.
Winter would come with snow and ice.
Then spring would return, the weather nice.
Going to school, moving to a new abode,
Were milestones along my personal life's road.
I don't think I was ever aware of death
'Til I experienced it seeing a pet draw its last breath.
The lesson is, life is finite. There will be a final page.
Changes will occur as we grow and age.
Sometime as a youth, I thought about a life's plan.
I would go through school and become a man.
I'd study engineering which seemed to be my bent.
I would fall in love with a young lady, heaven sent.
Marriage, a good job, a home, kids with my wife,
Then beyond that, vagueness in plans for my life.
I knew my kids would grow, have kids of their own,
Who in turn would become full grown.
I had no thoughts of retirement or growing old,
Having the occasional infirmity that would unfold.

Life has been an exciting journey looking back.
There were unforeseen paths along the track.
Graduate school was chosen for instance
When I received a letter, it seemed by chance.
I wasn't driven by ambition you see,
When I got my Masters of Science and PhD.
My Air Force assignment by chance was what I desired.
We found the town where we have lived, and now I'm retired.
Work has been satisfying. I've contributed a share.
I volunteered in many ways which means I care.
All these years I've loved my kids and my wife.
My great journey has been the very best life.
Except maybe for financial matters, I wouldn't change a thing.
I'm a common man but often feel a king.

26.The Herb Garden

I get a little down. The future isn't promising to me.
It clears up fast. A young girl shows me how to see.
By Victoria Hand, Age 12, Our Youngest Granddaughter
I tenderly water the
Herb garden and I
Carefully pull out all
The weeds and I
Put the fertilizer in
The dirt and I
Tenderly line the
Garden with animal proof
Fencing to protect the
Delicate plants I harvest the
Fully grown herbs like
A loving mother I

Smell the fresh scented leaves
Of the mint and I plant new
Herbs in the empty places
Like babies in cradles I
Carefully lift one of the rocks
On the cold stone path
I gently pick up the earth worm
And hold it in my hand and
I place it thankfully into the garden
And I watch it burrow under the soft
Soil that will be its home
Until the cold rain comes...

27. What a Wonderful World (Altered)*

They asked what was my favorite song.
With little thought I made my selection which can't be wrong.
It's composed of common words with simple ideas,
Sung with a gravelly voice which normally wouldn't please.
It has that endearing quality which for me is the best,
How ordinary folks can feel truly blest.
I've made alterations for the deaf and blind.
These don't change the meaning you will find.
For the hearing impaired, we need but two.
For the blind there was more to do.

I.   I see trees of green, red roses too.
        I see them bloom, for me and for you.
        And I think to myself, what a wonderful world.

II.   I see skies of blue, clouds of white.
        Bright blessed days, dark sacred nights.
        And I think to myself, what a wonderful world.

III.   The colors of a rainbow, so pretty in the sky,
        Are also on the faces of people going by.
        I see friends shaking hands, saying how do you do.
        They're really saying I love you.
        I see (hear) babies smile (cry), I watch them grow.
        Yes, I think to myself, what a wonderful world.
Repeat III.
I.   I hear wind in the trees, I smell flowers too.
        They're about to bloom, for me and for you.
        And I think to myself, what a wonderful world.
II.   I feel the rays of the sun, clouds shade the light.
        Warm blessed days, cool sacred nights.
        And I think to myself, what a wonderful world.
III.   The sounds of the birds, so pretty to hear.
        I love the voices, of people coming near.
        I hear friend greeting friend, saying how do you do,
        They're really saying I love you.
        I hear babies cry, I know how they grow.
        They'll learn much more, than I'll ever know.
        Yes, I think to myself, what a wonderful world.
*By Timothy J. Rice-Oxley, Etal. Sung by Louis
Armstrong